What people are saying about …

AHA

"Kyle knows where we live and where we could live with God's help. He is committed to helping us move in the right direction. If you need a helping hand in your journey, he'll point you to the right Person."

Max Lucado, pastor of Oak Hills
Church and author of *Grace*

"Kyle will challenge you to grow from a fair-weather fan to a full-time follower of Christ."

Craig Groeschel, senior pastor of
LifeChurch.tv and author of *Fight*

"Kyle will challenge even the most obedient Christians to relook at their relationship with Christ."

Mike Huckabee, former governor of
Arkansas and bestselling author

"Like his preaching, Kyle's writings will bring you face-to-face with areas you need to change and the One who has the power to change you."

Dave Stone, senior pastor of Southeast
Christian Church and author of
Raising Your Kids to Love the Lord

"Fresh, insightful, practical—Kyle's writing and teaching are helping countless people. I'm thrilled with how God is using him to challenge and encourage both Christians and those who are checking out the faith. Count me among his many fans!"

Lee Strobel, bestselling author and professor at Houston Baptist University

"AHA outlines biblical transformation and how it works in a simple yet profound way. Do you want to change, improve, or grow? You must get this book!"

Mark Batterson, lead pastor of National Community Church and *New York Times* bestselling author of *All In*

"Kyle cuts through all the nonsense and takes us straight to what is most important spiritually."

Jud Wilhite, senior pastor of Central Christian Church and author of *The God of Yes*

"If you're minimizing just how bad things have gotten in your life or are simply ready to change for good, then *AHA* awaits. This book is a gut punch to passivity. A bombshell to procrastination. Don't hold back now. Embrace the startling realization in these pages, talk straight with your soul, and take immediate action. Your gracious, loving Father stands ready for you."

Caleb Breakey, author of *Called to Stay* and *Dating Like Airplanes*

"Kyle is a great communicator, always driving home his messages in powerful, compelling, and practical ways."

David Novak, CEO of YUM! Brands
(Taco Bell, Pizza Hut, KFC) and
author of *Taking People with You*

AHA

AWAKENING.HONESTY.ACTION

THE GOD MOMENT THAT
CHANGES EVERYTHING

kyle idleman

David C Cook®

transforming lives together

AHA

Published by David C Cook
4050 Lee Vance View
Colorado Springs, CO 80918 U.S.A.

David C Cook Distribution Canada
55 Woodslee Avenue, Paris, Ontario, Canada N3L 3E5

David C Cook U.K., Kingsway Communications
Eastbourne, East Sussex BN23 6NT, England

The graphic circle C logo is a registered trademark of David C Cook.

The website addresses recommended throughout this book are offered as a
resource to you. These websites are not intended in any way to be or imply an
endorsement on the part of David C Cook, nor do we vouch for their content.

LCCN 2013955269
ISBN 978-0-781-41049-6
eISBN 978-1-4347-0751-2

© 2014 Kyle Idleman
Published in association with the literary agency of The
Gates Group, www.the-gates-group.com

The Team: Alex Field, Amy Konyndyk, Nick Lee, Tonya Osterhouse, Karen Athen
Cover Design: Amy Konyndyk
Cover Photo: Matt Garmany and Jennifer Wollen

Printed in the United States of America
First Edition 2014

1 2 3 4 5 6 7 8 9 10

122613

To my four children—Kenzie,
Morgan, Mason, and Kael
Your Father's arms are always open, and so are mine.

Special acknowledgment to Taylor Walling: Whether it's writing a song, a sermon, or a book, God has given you a gift with words. Thank you for all of your great help and hard work in putting this book together.

CONTENTS

Chapter 1

THE DISTANT COUNTRY

Quick tip: don't ask the bookstore clerk for directions to the self-help section.

Ironically, you're better off helping *yourself* find the self-help section. I recently made the mistake of walking into a bookstore and asking where the self-help section was located. The store clerk, initially disinterested and dazed, perked up and stared at me. I think he was trying to ascertain exactly what parts of my self needed help. I started to feel insecure, because I know there are plenty of ways my self needs help.

Finally, he pointed me toward a section in the back of the store that was actually like an entire region. In fact, I would say they had dedicated one-fourth of the store to all manner of self-help guides.

I perused the aisles, discovering new things about myself that needed help. There were titles like *How to Make People Like You in 90 Seconds or Less*, *Becoming a Better You*, and *Influence: The Psychology of Persuasion*. It was overwhelming. I fled the self-help section, doubts about my mental and physical health nipping at my heels.[1]

Most of these books promised a new and improved version of my life in a few easy steps. It's hard not to be cynical, because logically speaking, if one of the books worked, the rest of them wouldn't be necessary. But the truth is, self-help books that promise life transformation are everywhere.

An article in *New York* magazine reported that the self-help movement has mushroomed into an "$11 billion industry dedicated to telling us how to improve our lives."[2] The article reported there are at least 45,000 self-help books in print.

Despite these thousands of fix-it guides, most of us would readily admit we still need help. Survey the shelves of our bookstores. The most popular topics: diet and exercise, improving your marriage, getting control of your finances, stress management, and overcoming your addictions. And these books, despite their different topics and titles, have such similar taglines and formulas that when I walked around the self-help shelves, I felt like all the authors had been at the same Mad Libs party:

Follow our (PICK A NUMBER BETWEEN 1–8) *easy steps, and we guarantee you will* (INSERT FINANCIAL GAIN, WEIGHT LOSS GOAL,

---

1   Full disclosure: I purchased *3 Jedi Mind Tricks for Street Fighters*. You got a problem with that? (Mind trick number 1: Be an Aggressor.)

2   Kathryn Schulz, "The Self in Self-Help," *New York*, January 6, 2013, http://nymag.com/health/self-help/2013/schulz-self-searching/.

OR RELATIONAL STATUS) *in only a matter of* (PICK A NUMBER BETWEEN 1–5) (INSERT A MEASUREMENT OF TIME).

But because we are all too aware that our selves need help, we are often quick to jump on this misery merry-go-round of trying six steps to better our lives and expecting better results.

We know something is wrong.

We even know *what* we want to change.

Our diagnosis is spot-on, but no medication seems to do the trick.

If you picked up this book because you are trying to help yourself make significant changes, I want to tell you up front that this isn't the book for you. If self could help, then we would all have been fixed a long time ago.

So let me be clear: AHA is not a self-help process. It's the antithesis of a self-help book. What Bizarro is to Superman,[3] this book is to the self-help genre. **This journey begins with a rejection of your self's offer to help.**

---

3 If this reference didn't connect with you, please choose one of the following: what Screech is to Zack; what Shaggy is to Fred; what the Atkins diet is to Olive Garden; what Happy Gilmore is to Shooter McGavin; what Iceman is to Maverick; what the Fratellis are to the Goonies; what Newman is to Seinfeld; or what shirts are to Matthew McConaughey.

The Story of AHA

Instead of self-help, we are asking for God's help, because AHA is a spiritual experience that brings about supernatural change. More specifically, let's define the word *aha* this way: "a sudden recognition that leads to an honest moment that brings lasting change."

I love witnessing AHA. I see it almost every weekend at the church where I serve. I listen to people as they tell about the spiritual awakening they have experienced. In that moment there was a beautiful collision. At just the right time, a person's life collides with God's Word and the power of the Holy Spirit, and everything changes.

When Jesus taught about this spiritual transformation, He would most often tell stories. AHA can't be fully explained. There is a sense in which it has to be experienced to be understood. So it's through stories that AHA is best captured.

One woman told me about how she turned to impulsive eating to cope with life. For her, there was nothing a day could throw at her that she couldn't eat away. A stressful week of work would lead to a weekend of third and fourth helpings. Facing anxiety due to an upcoming project, she would bring home two or three desserts and eat them in one evening. Despite trying every self-help diet and exercise fad, she reached 325 pounds. This seemingly unstoppable weight gain put her at a point of dark depression, which only worsened her eating.

After months and months in the vicious cycle of binging and depression, she realized something: *food was never going to fill the emptiness in her heart.* She had been trying to satisfy her soul by feeding her stomach.

When she came to church, she heard a message from John 6 in which Jesus described Himself as the "Bread of Life." She suddenly realized that she had been trying to make food do for her what only Jesus can do.

That was four years and 170 pounds ago. But the outward change was really just a by-product of the inner transformation she experienced when her life collided with the gospel, and she started looking to Jesus to fill the emptiness of her heart.

AHA.

I was talking to a man whose life had been an ongoing struggle with alcoholism. He tried to make changes many times. He went through numerous self-help programs and had been through the twelve steps. They helped for a season, but he was never really on the wagon long enough to fall off.

Over the years, he realized how much his drinking cost him, but even when he thought he'd finally hit rock bottom, things managed to fall even farther. One day he was listening to a sermon, and the pastor was preaching from the passage where Paul says, "Do not get drunk on wine, which leads to debauchery. Instead, be filled with the Spirit" (Eph. 5:18). Immediately, this truth from God's Word opened his eyes: he had been looking to alcohol to do for him what the Holy Spirit was meant to do.

When he was down and depressed, he would drink for comfort and peace, but the Holy Spirit wanted to comfort him. When he was feeling insecure, he would drink and feel a sense of security and boldness, but the Holy Spirit wanted to fill him with courage and strength. When he was uncertain about the future and what he should do next, he would drink to help him cope, but the Holy Spirit wanted to guide and direct him in a new way.

AHA.

Though I have heard hundreds of AHA stories over the years, my favorite is the one Jesus tells in Luke 15. It's commonly known as the parable of the prodigal son. Charles Dickens famously called this parable "the greatest short story ever told." But while it's a parable and not a real-life story, it doesn't mean it isn't a story full of real life. It's almost impossible to read this story without finding yourself in it.

> There was a man who had two sons. The younger one said to his father, "Father, give me my share of the estate." So he divided his property between them.
>
> Not long after that, the younger son got together all he had, set off for a distant country and there squandered his wealth in wild living. After he had spent everything, there was a severe famine in that whole country, and he began to be in need. So he went and hired himself out to a citizen of that country, who sent him to his fields to feed pigs. He longed to fill his stomach with the pods that the pigs were eating, but no one gave him anything.
>
> When he came to his senses, he said, "How many of my father's hired servants have food to spare, and here I am starving to death! I will set out

and go back to my father and say to him: Father, I have sinned against heaven and against you. I am no longer worthy to be called your son; make me like one of your hired servants." So he got up and went to his father.

But while he was still a long way off, his father saw him and was filled with compassion for him; he ran to his son, threw his arms around him and kissed him.

The son said to him, "Father, I have sinned against heaven and against you. I am no longer worthy to be called your son."

But the father said to his servants, "Quick! Bring the best robe and put it on him. Put a ring on his finger and sandals on his feet. Bring the fattened calf and kill it. Let's have a feast and celebrate. For this son of mine was dead and is alive again; he was lost and is found." So they began to celebrate.

Meanwhile, the older son was in the field. When he came near the house, he heard music and dancing. So he called one of the servants and asked him what was going on. "Your brother has come," he replied, "and your father has killed the fattened calf because he has him back safe and sound."

The older brother became angry and refused to go in. So his father went out and pleaded with him. But he answered his father, "Look! All these years I've been slaving for you and never disobeyed your orders. Yet you never gave me even a young goat so I could celebrate with my friends. But when this son of yours who has squandered your property with prostitutes comes home, you kill the fattened calf for him!"

"My son," the father said, "you are always with me, and everything I have is yours. But we had to celebrate and be glad, because this brother of yours was dead and is alive again; he was lost and is found."

After studying this story in depth, I discovered that within this parable, there are three ingredients that are present in every AHA experience. So as we study this story together and travel with the Prodigal Son on his journey, we will identify the three ingredients of AHA in his life and pray for them in our own.

The Recipe for AHA

My wife has this cookbook at home, a gift from our wedding. It's called *The Three Ingredient Cookbook*. She would want me to tell you that she doesn't really use it. When she cooks, there's typically more than three ingredients involved. The truth is I'm the one who uses *The Three Ingredient Cookbook*.

On the rare occasions I'm allowed in the kitchen, this cookbook is my go-to cooking companion, because honestly, three ingredients is about my culinary capacity. One of the things I've learned the hard way is that when using *The Three Ingredient Cookbook*, all the ingredients are necessary—no, absolutely vital.

This is the downside to *The Three Ingredient Cookbook*. You can't cheat. If you use only two ingredients, it doesn't work very well.

The same is true for AHA.

I've listened to the AHA experiences of hundreds—if not thousands—of people over the years. I've studied numerous transformation experiences of key figures in the Bible. With striking consistency, AHA always has three ingredients. If any one of these ingredients is missing, it short-circuits the transformation process:

1. A Sudden Awakening
2. Brutal Honesty
3. Immediate Action

If there is an awakening and honesty, but no action, then AHA doesn't happen.

If there is awakening and action, but honesty is overlooked, AHA will be short-lived.

But when God's Word and the Holy Spirit bring these three things together in your life, you will experience AHA—a God-given moment that changes everything.

When I met Justin, he was desperate for AHA. He grew up in a Christian home and attended a Christian school. His parents kept his hair short and his curfew early. He became convinced that his sheltered life had caused him to miss out. One year, Justin sat at home watching *MTV Spring Break*, thinking about all the fun he should be having. So after he graduated from high school, he packed his bags and headed for a Distant Country.

A distant country is the generic description of where the Prodigal Son traveled after demanding his inheritance and leaving his father. The Jewish audience that listened to this parable understood that the "distant country" meant more than just a faraway place. Any distant land would be considered Gentile land. The implication was clear: the son wasn't just turning his back on his father; he was turning his back on his faith entirely. More than just walking away from his earthly father, we find that the Prodigal Son was walking away from his heavenly Father.

You Are Here

Have you ever been a little lost in a mall or maybe at an amusement park? You may have known where you were trying to go, but unless you knew where you were starting from, it was impossible to figure out how to get there. When you walked up to the giant map, the first thing you tried to figure out was not your future destination but your current location. Your eyes scanned the map looking for that familiar "YOU ARE HERE" symbol.

AHA begins with recognizing our current location. In one area or another, all of us are in the Distant Country. The *Distant Country* can be defined as any area of our lives where we have walked away from God. It may be that every part of you is living in the Distant Country, or it may just be a specific area of your life where you've left God out. No Trespassing signs line the perimeter and make it clear that God is not welcome.

It may help to pause here and identify areas of your own life that could be described as Distant Country. Take a moment and give a specific location for this general description. Write down the areas of your life where God is not welcome:

LIST YOUR DISTANT COUNTRY HERE

Father's
House

How we ended up where we are isn't always clear. There are many reasons why we leave the Father for the Distant Country, but the Bible says that all of us will find ourselves there at some point. Isaiah 59 explains that sin is what separates us from God. And Romans 3 tells us that all of us have sinned. Sin is the vehicle that every one of us has taken to the Distant Country.

Leaving the Father

I've discovered that what drives many travelers to the Distant Country is that they are running away from a god that doesn't exist. For one reason or another, their perception of God doesn't match up with reality. They are rejecting a god they created rather than the true God who created them.

Justin ran away from God and headed to the Distant Country because he was sure God was an **Unreasonable Father**. Like the son in Luke 15, Justin was convinced that staying with his father was causing him to miss out. In this light, God becomes an unreasonable Father who has a long list of rules that seem designed to take all the fun out of life. I've heard God described as "The Great Cosmic Killjoy." Many people pack their bags and head to the Distant Country because they are convinced that God's way is too restrictive and His path too narrow. They see God's boundaries as a fence that imprisons them rather than as a guardrail that protects them.

Justin grew up in a very religious home. One of the reasons Jesus wasn't a fan of religion is that religion reinforced rules using guilt and shame. And Justin joined the large caravan of travelers leaving the church in which they grew up to head to the Distant Country because they thought of God not just as an unreasonable Father but as an **Unpleasable Father**. The rationale goes something like this: "Because God's standards are so high, nothing I do will ever be good enough for Him. So why stick around and try?"

Maybe you grew up in a church that perpetuated this belief. Whenever you heard about God in church, He always seemed frustrated with you. Everything you heard about Him made you believe that whenever He looked at you, He shook His head in disappointment. His rules and expectations were unreasonable, and no matter how much effort you made, God never seemed to be pleased.

Maybe you grew up feeling like your best was never good enough for God. You brought home a B on your report card, but it should have been an A. If you scored fifteen points in the basketball game, you should've scored twenty.

If you think of God as an impossible-to-please Father, at some point you will quit trying to please Him altogether. What's the point of making the effort if nothing you do is good enough?

Some leave the Father and head for the Distant Country because they see God as an **Unmerciful Father**. They see God as an angry Father who is borderline abusive and seems to find pleasure in distributing punishment. He's always watching and waiting for you to slip up, and when He catches you, it won't matter how sorry you are—there will be hell to pay—*literally*. If you were taught to fear God, then you would naturally respond to Him by running away.

A few years ago, I came home from work to find that my wife and kids had agreed to dog-sit for friends of ours. The dog's name was Pork Chop, and everyone was excited about our new houseguest. But the first time I walked into the room, Pork Chop was not glad to see me. He responded to my presence by peeing on the floor and running into the next room. I tried not to take it too personally, but later that same evening, when I walked into the room where Pork Chop was, he responded the same way. He peed, ran away, and hid.

We later found out that Pork Chop's owners had rescued him from an abusive situation where he'd learned to be afraid of men. He had no reason to fear me—I had taken this dog into my home and provided food and shelter for him—but because he had learned to be afraid of men, he would always run away, and I could never get close to him.

That's how some people relate to God.[4] They run away to the Distant Country and never give Him a chance, because they've been conditioned to be afraid of Him.

And finally, I've talked to many travelers who are in the Distant Country because they see God as an **Uncaring Father**. They feel like God wasn't there for them when they needed Him the most, so they struck out for the Distant Country and didn't look back. From then on, they perceived God to be an impersonal force that didn't know or care about what was happening in their lives.

Their relationship with God can be summed up like this: "If He doesn't care about me, then I don't care about Him."

Family therapist John Trent once shared a letter given to him by a third-grade teacher. The letter was part of an assignment she'd given students, asking them to write a letter to their fathers.

Here's a letter one girl wrote:

Dear Daddy, I love you so much. When are you going to come see me again? I miss you very much. I love when you take me to the pool. When am I going to spend the night at your house? Have you ever seen my house before? I want to see what your house looks like. When am I going to get to see you again? I love you, Daddy.

What is going to happen to that third-grader's heart as she gets older? As it concerns her father, she will become more disillusioned and disappointed, and eventually she may even become bitter and wounded. At the very least, it's unlikely she'll stick around. Chances

---

4   Minus the peeing.

are, she'll pack her bags and head out to the Distant Country and leave her father behind.

Our Real Heavenly Father

Whatever caused someone to leave the Father and head to the Distant Country, they will inevitably find themselves in a place where they are in desperate need of help. The kind of help that self can't give. What we'll discover in the parable is that even though we turned our back on God and walked away, He is a loving, merciful, gracious, and caring Father who wants to do more than just help us—He wants to save us.

Justin was sitting at home watching MTV, convinced he was missing out and ready to get out there and really live. After heading to the Distant Country, Justin embraced wild living—sex, booze, parties, and all-nighters. Justin got wildest when it came to drugs: you name it; he tried it. It didn't matter how extreme or how danger-ous; he was always ready to get high.

After a while, the drugs he enjoyed as recreation became an addiction, and it brought Justin to his knees. With his life in shambles, Justin made some noble attempts at self-help, but each tearful resolution always ended in relapse.

Then Justin tried to get professional help. Rehab treatments failed, addiction cleanses didn't stick, and working a program never really worked. Justin started to feel like he had nowhere to turn. A horrifying notion awoke inside of him: *maybe I'm broken for good.*

Then, one weekend after church, he tracked me down. I'll never forget the first words out of his mouth: "I'm high on heroin right now."

Looking into his sunken face and bloodshot eyes, I believed him. He began to weep as he told me his story. It seemed that his reckless choices had left a trail of emotional wreckage that had wounded his relationships with friends, family, and ultimately, God.

Justin came to realize that God didn't want to ruin life's fun; rather, He was a Father who loved him and would forgive him no matter what. Justin said he felt he needed to get help *that instant*, because he couldn't trust himself to wait the twenty-four hours until Monday. He looked at me, shaken by his own reality, desperate for help. Justin put it to me this way: "I have no other place to turn and nowhere else to go. There is nothing I can do to help myself. Will you ask God to help me?"

That's where the AHA journey begins. Not with a determined commitment to self-help but with a humble request for God's help.

PART 1
SUDDEN AWAKENING

He came to his senses…

Chapter 2

COMING TO YOUR SENSES

Not long ago, one of my daughters set my iPhone alarm ringtone to match that of her favorite animal. It's labeled "Horses Neighing." It should be called "Death by Stampede."

At 5:30 in the morning, my alarm went off, and I shot straight up in bed, wide-awake, a stampede charging through my bedroom. While changing it back to my standard alarm, I noticed a wide array of other options. If you use an iPhone, go ahead and pull it out right now. Tap on "Settings," then "Sounds," then "Ringtones." Try tapping on "Doorbell." That could be confusing. *What's happening? Am I supposed to wake up? Is someone here to see me?* Not the best way to start off your day.

Some of the sounds wouldn't do anything to get me out of bed, like the one labeled "Harp." It trills a soft melody, and just listening to it makes me sleepy. I feel as though it's singing to me, "Go back to sleep. It's the right thing to do. Your boss will understand." If this gentle tune were my regular alarm, that's exactly what I'd do every morning.

I've found that the most effective alarm ringtone for me is labeled "Old Car Horn." If you don't have an iPhone, think in terms of a house alarm that you can hear on the other side of the neighborhood. Now imagine that you are sleeping inside the speaker. It's a highly effective alarm. And the great thing is that this alarm has a unique backup system that's almost fail proof. If the alarm doesn't get me out of bed immediately, the backup system kicks into gear—literally. My wife's foot will slam into the small of my back, urging me to get out of bed to shut the alarm off.

But here's what I've discovered: the effectiveness of the alarm is in direct correlation to how much you don't want to hear it.

In other words, until your desire not to hear the alarm outweighs your desire to keep sleeping—you're not going to wake up.

Similarly, a sudden awakening takes place when God finally gets our attention. The alarm sounds, and this time we hear it. The alarm causes us to sit up and get out of bed. We immediately become aware of our present circumstances and the reality that something must change. Though we've traveled far from the Father and are living in the Distant Country, we awake to reality like never before. This is the first ingredient of AHA—a sudden awakening. The Prodigal Son experienced this in Luke 15:17. It reads:

When he came to his senses …

He sat straight up and suddenly realized what his life had become. He wondered how things had turned out this way. When he'd left his father's house, he'd never imagined it would have come to this. This was never part of the plan. But now life had his attention, and he knew things had to change. One moment he was sleeping, the next he was awake.

AHA.

Have you ever had a moment like this?

Sudden Awakenings

A man struggled with gambling—not just for a season, but for a lifetime. It started in college, where late-night poker games slowly got out of hand. After a month-long losing streak with his buddies, he grew determined to win. After losing his money, he bet the worth of his class textbooks, much to his friends' protests.

The alarm first sounded when his friends refused to play with him anymore, but he didn't hear it. Instead, he turned to new avenues with willing players.

He always lost more than he made, but nothing thrilled him like the roll of dice or a new hand of cards. Eventually his debts mounted, and the alarm sounded again when he was forced to drop out of college.

He managed to keep his gambling a secret, marrying a woman who was only vaguely aware that he liked to play card games every now and then. But one weekend when she was out of town, he tore through his cash reserves in a betting fever and eventually withdrew two grand from their checking account. The alarm got a little louder when, upon returning from her trip, his wife discovered what he'd done and left the house without even unpacking her bag. She stayed at her sister's for a month, only returning after he agreed to her ultimatum.

The alarm sounded again.

He joined a support group, and it helped for a while. He tried to work the program, but he continued to struggle. Even watching ESPN was a temptation for him to place a few bets online, and with sports happening year-round, he couldn't escape it.

This past year, he lost his job and went back to the casino. One night he returned home to find a note from his wife. This time, it seems, may have been the last straw.

The alarm sounds.

A wife in her mid-thirties returned home after meeting up with her high-school sweetheart. She'd recently reconnected with him on Facebook. She'd been friend requesting a bevy of old classmates, and one day when she checked her page, he had posted to say hi.

Through private messages, they relived some old memories. Eventually, one of them suggested they meet up. They met in the lobby of a hotel, and when he first walked up, she'd felt a flurry of emotions. They ate lunch together, and he was still charming, still funny. At one point in the meal, he passed the salt, and their hands brushed against each other. Her heart beat furiously, as though she were a schoolgirl all over again. She suddenly felt so alive, like she hadn't in a long time.

As she walked in the door of her home, she bumped into a table and knocked over a family photo. Setting it back up, she took a moment to look at the picture of herself with her husband and their three children. They were all making funny faces at the camera.

The alarm sounds.

A college student's grades came in the mail. His partying resulted in him flunking out of school.

She's a junior in high school, and with trembling hands, she held a pregnancy test as she waited for the result.

He logged off the website, deleted his history, and turned off the computer. His wife slept in the other room, but he had chosen this over her.

Sooner or later in the Distant Country, *the alarm will sound.*

Heavy Sleeper

The son in Luke 15 didn't hear the alarm until he made it to the pigpen.

He didn't hear it when he made his request to his father asking for his share of the inheritance. He was basically saying, "Dad, I can't wait for you to die. I want the money now."

He didn't hear the alarm when, after a few raging weekends in the Distant Country, his wallet felt much lighter.

He didn't even hear it when a famine swept through the land.

He didn't hear it when he found himself taking on the job of pig-sitter.

It's hard not to read this story and ask yourself: "How did he not hear the alarm? How could he sleep through that?"

Often we miss the alarms sounding in our lives because we're not sensitive to them. The harp won't do the job—it's going to take the threat of death by stampede to wake us up. So instead of responding to the alarm early, we keep hitting snooze. The alarm grows louder and louder until eventually it is so unpleasant that we can't ignore it any longer. So we wake up, rub our eyes, look around to find pigs surrounding us, and wonder how it came to this.

Here's my question for you: Are there alarms sounding in your life right now?

In Scripture there are a number of examples of how God sounds the alarm. Oftentimes the alarm sounds early on to wake us up before things have fallen apart. Sometimes people think they have to hit rock bottom before they come to their senses, but what if God is trying to wake you up right now to save you from heartbreak in the Distant Country later?

Second Chronicles 36:15 speaks of how God sounds the alarm to warn His people:

> And the LORD God of their fathers sent *warnings* to
> them by His messengers, rising up early and send-
> ing *them* … (NKJV)

The expression *rising up early* doesn't mean God got out of bed early. Rather, it is best understood as "taking action early." In this context, it means He sounded the alarm as quickly as the problems were perceived. And then we read why He warned:

> … because He had compassion on His people …

This is yet another way that God is a loving Father. The moment a parent perceives their child to be in danger, they warn the child of the coming consequences.

A few years ago my family visited my parents' house for the holidays. They live on a quiet cul-de-sac where cars rarely come down the street. One day my then-four-year-old son, Kael, was riding his Big Wheel down the driveway. I stepped outside and saw a car coming down the street pretty fast. Kael needed to be warned that the car was coming.

I didn't think, *I've got a good thirty seconds before that car makes contact with my son. That's enough time to check my texts before I say something.*

I didn't smile and say, "Hey, buddy, there's a Ford SUV coming right for you. You might want to think about slowing down."

With a sense of urgency, I yelled, "Kael, stop right now!"

As soon as I perceived the danger, I warned him. That's what a loving father does.

Throughout Scripture, we read some different ways that God rises up early to sound the alarm:

1. His Word at just the right time

In Genesis 4, God sounded the first individual, timely, specific alarm.

The story is familiar enough. Adam and Eve had two sons at the time—Cain and Abel. Likely this story is one you're somewhat familiar with, but there is a warning to Cain in this story that I had never noticed before.

In Genesis 4:2–5, it says this:

> Now Abel kept flocks (so he is a shepherd), and
> Cain worked the soil (he is a farmer). In the course
> of time Cain brought some of the fruits of the soil
> as an offering to the LORD. And Abel also brought
> an offering—fat portions from some of the first-
> born of his flock. The LORD looked with favor on
> Abel and his offering, but on Cain and his offering
> he did not look with favor. So Cain was very angry,
> and his face was downcast. (parentheses mine)

You've got Abel, who was obedient to God's command and
brought his firstfruits. He brought a portion of the best of what he
had, and he gave it to God as an offering. But Cain didn't do that.
Cain gave God the leftovers.

Well, when God saw this, He accepted Abel's offering and
blessed him, but He rejected Cain's offering, and Cain got discouraged about it. Cain was jealous of his brother. He was angry. He
was upset. Cain, the world's first son, was on the prodigal path to
the Distant Country. God saw what was happening and sounded
the alarm.

In verses 6–7, it says:

> Then the LORD said to Cain, "Why are you angry?
> Why is your face downcast? If you do what is right,
> will you not be accepted?"

God, as a Father, said, "Listen close. It's not too late. I know
right now you're feeling discouraged. I know my response wasn't

what you wanted. I know things haven't really turned out the way you had hoped, but *it's not too late*. You still have an opportunity here to do the right thing. If you'll just do the right thing, even though you don't feel like it, everything will be okay."

Then God issued a second alarm:

> But if you do not do what is right, sin is crouching
> at your door; it desires to have you, but you must
> rule over it.

Draw a line under this phrase: "sin is crouching at your door."

God painted a picture of Cain getting ready to open up a door, but if he opened it, he would find that on the other side of that door was a decision that would destroy his family and devastate his life. God the Father saw the first son going toward the door, and He put a heavy hand on the door. He held it shut for a moment and, in essence, said, "Now wait a minute, Cain. Push Pause. You need to take a deep breath, and you need to recognize something. What is right behind this door, what is just a moment away for you, has the power to destroy. It seeks to have you. Cain, you need to be really careful with what you do next."

And the alarm sounded as God stepped back and let Cain choose for himself. Just like the father in Luke 15, God was not going to force His child to make the right decision. Any parent knows that as much as you may want to have that kind of control, eventually, the kids have to decide for themselves.

Ultimately, Cain ignored the alarms and opened the door. Verse 8 says:

> Now Cain said to his brother Abel, "Let's go out
> to the field." While they were in the field, Cain
> attacked his brother Abel and killed him.

So God rose early and warned Cain that the path he was on was going to lead to destruction. At just the right moment, He spoke into Cain's life and said, "Look, sin is crouching right outside your door. You need to be on guard." But Cain didn't hear it. He sleepwalked through the alarm, and everything came crashing down around him.

In hindsight, most of us can identify such moments in our lives. God sounded the alarm, but we rolled over and went back to sleep.

As I have listened to people's AHA stories over the years, one of the questions I often ask is: Looking back, can you see how God tried to get your attention even though you didn't realize it?

A man getting ready to divorce his wife went to church and the preacher started the sermon with these words: "I am going to say something that will make some of you uncomfortable because you don't think God hates anything, but the Bible says, 'God hates divorce.'" The man got up and walked out.

Years later, after a painful divorce, he went back and got a recording of that sermon. He listened as the preacher explained that just as a father hates cancer because of what it does to his child, so God hates divorce because of what it does to His children. The man told me he wept as he listened to the warnings in the sermon, because he felt like the preacher was describing what had since happened to his life and family.

A senior in high school was dating a guy who didn't share her faith. She reasoned to herself that in time he would come around. When things started to get more serious, the leader of her small group pulled her aside and warned her about what the Bible says concerning such relationships. She listened and nodded, but inwardly she rolled her eyes.

That was six years ago. Now she has two kids and is married to a man who has never prayed with her and sleeps in on Sundays when she gets the kids up to go to church.

As a preacher, I am completely convinced that part of the supernatural power of God's Word is that it often intersects with our lives when we are most desperate for the truth. Like a GPS system that gives us a heads up when our exit is quickly approaching, God's Word speaks into our lives right when we need it the most.

2. The words of someone in your life

The alarm that can at times be most effective in our lives is the words of someone with whom we share life. The Prodigal Son needed a friend like this, but in the Distant Country, I'm sure they were hard to find.

Proverbs 27:6 says, "Wounds from a friend can be trusted." And sometimes, in emergency life situations, a familiar voice speaking truth into your life is exactly what you need, but it's rarely what you want.

In Galatians 2, Paul writes about the time when his friend and fellow apostle Peter withdrew from the Gentiles, because he was afraid of criticism from the Jews. Paul records in Galatians 2:11 how he handled this:

> When Cephas [Peter] came to Antioch, I opposed
> him to his face, because he stood condemned.

A good friend will sound the alarm. They don't want to share it, and you don't want hear it, but it's the only way you'll wake up.

Not long ago I came to work wearing an outfit that I convinced myself was cool. I wore a red polo shirt, pleated khaki pants, and white Nikes. When I walked into the office, a friend of mine took a quick glance at what I was wearing and said, "Hey, Zack Morris, how do you like working at Target?" From now on, whenever my fashion choices revert back to the early 90s, this friend just calls me Zack.[1]

We all need a friend like that from time to time. A friend who will tell us when we're neglecting our family for our work. A friend who will say something when our spending gets out of control. A friend who will challenge us to do more than just come to church a few weekends a month. A friend who will question a new relationship we're beginning.

---

1   For my fellow Gen Xers: Come to think of it, you can evaluate bad fashion by using the entire cast of *Saved by the Bell*. If someone is wearing stone-washed pleated jeans, you can call them A. C. Slater. If their pants are too high and their shirts too loud, you can call them Screech Powers. If their bangs are too big, you can them Kelly Kipowski. If they are twenty years old and dress like they're fifty, you can call them Lisa Turtle. And if whatever they wear, they still annoy you, you can call them Jessie Spano.

3. Future consequences

Another alarm for us is sometimes a sampling of future consequences. Sometimes God will give us a taste of the coming consequences of current actions—like a parking-lot fender bender that may save us from a five-car interstate pileup later, or a bounced check that will keep us from uncontrollable debt down the road. God will allow us to experience a sampling of what we can expect if we don't wake up.

A lot of us can mistake this alarm as a coincidental inconvenience. If the sampling of consequence isn't big enough or painful enough to get our attention, we often miss it. But as you look back on your life, I'm betting you could point out some times when God was trying to get your attention.

In the 80s and 90s, there was a TV show called *Scared Straight*. The show would take juvenile offenders—sixteen-year-old car thieves, high-school vandals, repeat-offender shoplifters—and put them in prison for a day.

Looking at the opening shots of these kids, the idea sounded a little cruel at first, but then I watched the interviews with these teens *before* they went into prison. They were obnoxiously arrogant. Smiles crossed their faces as they bragged about how easy the day would be. They were oblivious to the reality of the prison environment. In an interview, some of the police involved with the program told the show's producers how these kids thought prison actually sounded nice—like they could eat, sleep, and hang out all day for free.

As the kids walked into the prison, they put on orange jumpsuits. Throughout the day, they worked in the kitchen doing dishes and interacted with some truly terrifying convicts. The cameras zoomed in on these teenagers' faces, their cavalier claims long gone. I could see that they were starting to come to their senses. The alarm was sounding, and they were starting to hear it.

The show received some criticism, but I think we can all agree that one hard day in prison now is better than years behind bars later. And it turns out that for most of the kids on the show, it really did scare them straight. Less than 10 percent of the original cast ever went to prison. But there were a few who ended up in those orange jumpsuits as convicted felons doing hard time. And maybe you can relate to the regret they probably now experience as they sit in their cells looking back on their opportunity to change course.

4. The example of others before us

Another alarm that God can send our way is the example of people who've gone before us.

If you study the life of Cain in Scripture, you'll find his name is mentioned several times in the New Testament, and it's always used as a bad example. In other words, Cain becomes an alarm to wake up readers of the New Testament. The New Testament writers point to Cain and say to the rest of us, "Look, be careful of following Cain's path, because if you do, here's what will happen to you." Let me give you two examples of this from the New Testament:

> Do not be like Cain, who belonged to the evil one
> and murdered his brother. (1 John 3:12)

> Woe to them! They have taken the way of Cain.
> (Jude v. 11)

Scripture points to Cain as an example of what will happen if we ignore the alarm and continue down the path to the Distant Country. In fact, the Bible is surprisingly candid in sharing the stories of people who end up in the Distant Country. When we witness what others experience away from the Father's house, it's an alarm inviting us to come to our senses before we go any farther.

A number of years ago, I took my family on a month-long mission trip to the Dominican Republic. One of the challenges we had as parents was keeping our daughter away from the wild dogs that roamed the streets. What squirrels are to America, dogs are to the Dominican Republic. They are everywhere.

When my daughter was in second grade, she was the ultimate animal lover, and she could not keep her hands off these mangy dogs. We'd be walking through a market, and I'd turn around to see her softly petting a wild mutt. I often had to scoop her up in my arms before she extended her cheek to them for doggy kisses.

As parents, my wife and I tried very hard to help our daughter understand how serious this was. But throughout the trip, she kept getting in trouble for trying to love on these dangerous dogs. My little girl couldn't help herself. She has a tender heart, so she was especially drawn to the sickly looking ones—flea-ridden dogs with open wounds and weeping scabs.

One night after we said prayers, she said, "Dad, after we help all the people, can we help the dogs? I want to buy some bandages so we can fix them up." It was breaking her heart, but it was also a serious danger she was failing to recognize.

I knew I had to get her attention. So one morning, I woke up early and got online. I looked up video footage of hospitalized children who'd been bitten by rabid dogs. The videos were graphic and sobering. When my daughter awoke, I brought her to the laptop, and I showed her the clips of these injured children.[2] As I played the clips, I said, "Look, I've talked to you about this. I warned you about these dogs. You've been getting in trouble for it, but you're not staying away from them. You need to see what happened to other children who did what you're doing."

As she watched the video, I could see it in her eyes. The alarm sounded. There is something about seeing someone experience the consequences of decisions we're currently making that can help us come to our senses.

If you are on the path to the Distant Country, step back and ask yourself: Where is it leading? What happened to others who have gone this way? How has it worked out for the coworker who wasn't honest with his expense report? How has it worked out for the neighbor who thought she could fool around without her husband noticing? How has it worked out for the classmate who tried to cheat on the exam? How has it worked out for the businesswoman who put in overtime through the holidays and prioritized work over her family?

---

2   As I wrote that for you, I realized it was a questionable parenting tactic. But it
    worked!

Their experiences can serve as a warning to you: if you keep going down this path, you are going to end up in the same place.

Prayer for the Sleeping to Awake

One of my favorite Old Testament stories is found in the book of 2 Kings, where the king of Aram, an enemy of Israel, sent a great army to surround one of Israel's cities and destroy God's prophet, Elisha.

Elisha was with his servant when the enemy attacked, and the two of them were surrounded. The servant was terrified and cried out to Elisha. My guess is that he cried out with a sense of sheer panic, saying to Elisha, "Master! What are we going to do?"

Elisha responded with a remarkable statement. He said, "Don't be afraid.... Those who are with us are more than those who are with them" (2 Kings 6:16).

Elisha's servant looked around, but there was no one with them! They were all alone. It was the two of them against an army. Then Elisha prayed a simple prayer for his servant. He prayed: "Open his eyes, LORD, so that he may see."

Then we're told, "The LORD opened the servant's eyes, and he looked and saw the hills full of horses and chariots of fire all around Elisha" (2 Kings 6:17). His eyes were opened and ... aha—he suddenly realized that heavenly forces protected them and there had been nothing to fear in the first place.

And the prayer Elisha prayed for his servant is my prayer for you today.

God, open her eyes, and let her see that though he walked out on her, you will never leave her, and she is not alone.

God, open his eyes, so he can see his wife is cold and hard only because she doesn't feel safe enough to be vulnerable with him.

God, open his eyes that he may see he is living his life to impress others and glorify himself, which leads only to emptiness.

God, open her eyes, and let her see that a beautifully decorated and well-kept house has become more important to her than a joyful and peaceful home.

God, open his eyes, and let him see the single mom who lives next door with a young son who doesn't know how to throw a football.

God, open our eyes, and let us see the hungry and the hurting living just a few miles down the road.

God, open our eyes, and let us see the pride that has blinded us, the sin that has hardened us, and the lies that have deceived us.

Lord, we pray for AHA. Awaken us.

Chapter 3

A DESPERATE MOMENT

I'm not sure what comes to mind when you hear the phrase *rude awakening*. Perhaps you remember when you were awakened by a ringing phone in the middle of the night only to find out it was a wrong number. Parents, maybe you're remembering when you woke up in the middle of the night to find your creepy kid standing at the side of the bed staring at you, because apparently he thought it would be rude to wake you.

Thanks to youtube.com, you can now watch rude awakenings taken to a whole new level. Here are some of my favorite rude awakenings:

> Shaving cream and a feather
> Hot sauce on the lips
> Blanket exchanged for a roll of Bubble Wrap
> Air horn and Silly String
> Saran wrapped to the bed

Hot wax and a shirtless, hairy man sleeping on his
stomach[1]

Say what you will about rude awakenings, one thing is certain—
they are effective. The person is sound asleep one moment and as
wide-awake as one can get the next.

In Luke 15, the Prodigal Son headed to what Jesus called a distant
country. The Distant Country is any area of our lives where we are
trying to live independently of the Father. Initially the Prodigal Son
seemed to be having fun. The Bible says he spent all his money on wild
living. But eventually, life lived apart from the father fell apart.

Life got hard.

The Prodigal Son ran out of money, and then a famine hit the
land. One moment it was wild living, and the next he was trying to
survive. He found himself in such desperate need, Jesus said, "He
longed to fill his stomach with the pods that the pigs were eating."

Then he came to his senses.

The challenges and hardships of life have a way of getting our attention. Sometimes the only thing that will wake us up is a *rude* awakening.

I Stopped Running from God When ...

I asked my Facebook friends to finish this sentence for me: I stopped
running from God when ...

---

1   Fine, go ahead and watch a few. But when you find yourself watching "The
    Evolution of Dance" for the thirty-seventh time, let that be a reminder that you
    were reading this book.

Here are some of the responses I got:

I stopped running from God when ...
>   ... it became clear that I had made a mess of things.
>   ... I hit rock bottom.
>   ... she filed for divorce.
>   ... I heard myself say the words *I'm an alcoholic.*
>   ... people found out my secret.
>   ... the pregnancy test came pack positive.
>   ... the path I was on came to a dead end.
>   ... I woke up in a hospital after an overdose.
>   ... I was in the back of a police car.
>   ... I was fired for embezzlement.
>   ... the affair was discovered on July 4, 2009.
>   ... I realized I had nowhere else to go.

One way or another, most of them described a pigpen moment. God often uses desperate moments to wake us up. Only when things start to fall apart do we finally open our eyes.

Difficult Circumstances

It's worth noting that there are primarily two ways we arrive at a desperate moment. Here are the two categories that most desperate moments fit into:

1. Difficult circumstances
2. Deserved consequences

We find the son in Luke 15 experiencing both. He experienced some difficult circumstances:

> "... there was a severe famine in that whole country ..."
> (v. 14)

While there is never a good time for a famine, the timing couldn't have been worse for the Prodigal Son. He had done nothing to cause the famine. He had no control over the famine. It wasn't his fault, but at the worst possible moment, he found himself living through some difficult circumstances.

The audience that heard Jesus tell this story would have known all too well the horrors and devastation of a famine. They were common enough during the time of Jesus. Like me, most of you who are reading this have no idea what starvation feels like. The book of 2 Kings records the details of a famine in Samaria so devastating that people would buy dove dung to eat. We read about two mothers who were so desperate, they agreed to cook and eat their own babies.

So when Jesus spoke of a famine in the land, the crowd would have understood just how difficult things were for the Prodigal Son. But it was only when things got really hard that the son finally had a spiritual awakening.

I've heard enough AHA stories to know that this tends to be the norm rather than the exception. None of us would choose to go through tough times; but if we are honest, most of us in hindsight would admit that our AHA moments have most often come in the midst of difficult circumstances.

Erasing Famines

Recently I read about an experiment done by psychologist Jonathan Haidt. He came up with a fascinating hypothetical exercise. Participants were handed a summary of a person's life and asked to read it over. The summary looked something like this:

> Jillian will be born in August. As she grows, Jillian will develop a learning disability that will prevent her from learning to read at the appropriate age. Due to this disability, she will struggle with school for the rest of her years as a student. Despite her best efforts, her grades will always be average. In high school, Jillian will become best friends with a girl named Megan. They will share secrets and be nearly inseparable for much of their junior year. But Megan will be diagnosed with a rare, aggressive form of cancer, and she will pass away just as senior year begins. Jillian will mourn the loss, and her grades will suffer for it.
>
> She will attend a local community college, working a job and taking a small course load. The two-year program will take her three-and-a-half years to complete, and just before heading to a state school, Jillian will be involved in a drunk-driving accident. A drunk driver will hit her from behind, pushing her car into an intersection,

where a family of three will swerve to avoid her. They will skid off the road, hit a tree, and their youngest son will die. Though the fault isn't hers, Jillian will blame herself for his death and spiral into a deep depression.

Eventually, she will make it to a state school, finish her degree, and get a job working for a food distributor. She will love her job. Just as a promotion comes her way, an economic downturn will force the company to lay off much of their management, which now includes Jillian. In the devastated economic climate, Jillian will struggle to get work, and eventually she will file for bankruptcy, selling her house and moving into a small studio apartment to make ends meet. Though she will strive to get back on her feet, the economy will make it increasingly hard to do so, and she'll spend a few years living month to month.

She will eventually find another job, but due to her bankruptcy and season of unemployment, she won't be able to retire the way she thought she would, nor will she ever make as much as she used to. She will have to work hard into her old age, piecing her life back together.[2]

---

2   John Ortberg. "Don't Waste a Crisis," *Leadership Journal, Christianity Today Library*, January 31, 2011, http://www.ctlibrary.com/le/2011/winter/dontwastecrisis.html.

Here's the next part of the exercise: participants were asked to imagine that Jillian was their daughter. This was her unavoidable life story. She hasn't been born yet, but she would be soon, and this was where her life was headed. Participants then had five minutes to edit her story. Eraser in hand, they could eliminate whatever they wanted out of her life.

The question for participants was: What do you erase first?

Most of us would instinctively and frantically begin to erase the learning disability and the car accident and the financial challenges. We love our children and would want them to live a life without those hardships, pains, and setbacks. We would all prefer our children's lives be free from pain and anguish.

But ask yourself: Is that really what's best?

Do we really think a privileged life of smooth sailing is going to make our kids happy? What if you erase a difficult circumstance that will wake them up to prayer? What if you erase a hardship that's going to show them how to be joyful in spite of any circumstance? What if you erase some pain and suffering that ends up being the catalyst God uses in their life to cause them to cry out to Him? What if you erase a difficult circumstance that wakes them up to God's purpose for their lives?

It may sound harsh to say, but the number-one contributor to spiritual growth is not sermons, books, or small groups; the number-one contributor to spiritual growth is *difficult circumstances.* I can tell you this because of personal experience, reading spiritual-growth surveys, and my own anecdotal evidence after talking to thousands of people over the years. AHA comes out of the suffering, setbacks, and challenges of life. Many people could point to those moments as their greatest moments of spiritual awakening.

My friend Lori lost her seventeen-year-old daughter in a tragic car accident. Six weeks later, her son deployed to Iraq. No one is prepared to lose a child, but then to face the overwhelming fear of losing another child who is going off to fight a war ... This was Lori's worst nightmare. What made things even worse was that Lori and her husband had been separated for the previous year. In spite of her friends' and family's best efforts, she felt utterly alone. In this desperate moment, she came to realize that the only one who could hear her heart was God. She felt like she had no other choice and nowhere else to go, so she went back to church. Her first weekend in church, she worshipped God with tears streaming down her face. Before her world came crashing down around her, she didn't have much time for God, but in her desperation, she began crying out to Him every day.

As she shared her story with me, there were still tears, but these were tears of relief as she spoke of God's redeeming power. He gave her a renewed sense of purpose. She and her husband recommitted their lives to Christ and each other. Her son recently returned from Iraq and got married.

As painful as that season of life was for her, she looks back and sees it as a time of incredible spiritual awakening. In Proverbs 20:30, the Bible basically says it sometimes takes a painful experience to make us change our ways. And sometimes it does.

Sometimes it takes cancer to awaken us to things of eternal value.

Sometimes it takes unemployment to awaken us to a deeper prayer life.

Sometimes it takes a broken heart for us to finally let Jesus in.

Difficult circumstances don't always wake us up; sometimes they cause us to turn over, cover our heads with a pillow, and go back to sleep. Disappointment in life will often bring about one of two very different responses: we will either cry out to God in desperation, or we will distance ourselves from God. We may say, "Well, God isn't holding up His end of the deal. Look at the hand I've been dealt. This isn't the way my life was supposed to turn out. If God isn't going to be there for me, then I'm not going to be there for Him."

In the Old Testament book of Job, Satan was betting that Job would respond to difficult circumstances by distancing himself from God. Job was living what most of us would call the good life. Job 1:2–3 reads:

> He had seven sons and three daughters, and he owned seven thousand sheep, three thousand camels, five hundred yoke of oxen and five hundred donkeys, and had a large number of servants.

From there we read of one difficult circumstance after another. He lost his children when a strong wind collapsed a house on top of them. In chapter 2 Job was afflicted with painful sores from the soles of his feet to the top of his head. He lost everything. His wealth, his children, his health—it all disappeared. His wife had seen enough. In 2:9, she said to him, "Are you still maintaining your integrity? Curse God and die!" But in the midst of the pain, Job experienced an awakening. At the end of the book, he said to God, "My ears had heard of you but now my eyes have seen you."

AHA.

In the midst of the pain, Job saw God more clearly. The alarm sounded, his eyes were opened, and in his disappointment, he didn't distance himself from God; instead, he drew nearer.

Redeeming the Pain

Right now someone is reading this who is experiencing difficult circumstances. In your pain and disappointment, there is a part of you that wants to turn from God and walk away. But don't waste the pain. Hear the alarm and wake up.

In 2 Corinthians 7:10 we read, "For God sometimes uses sorrow in our lives to help us turn away from sin and seek eternal life" (LB). It doesn't say "God causes"; it says "God uses," and He wants to use these circumstances to draw you closer to Him.

Recently, while driving, I caught part of a radio interview with a guy named Gerald Sittser, a professor at Whitworth University.

A number of years ago, Gerald was in a car accident. He and some members of his family were in their minivan when a drunk driver slammed into them. In the accident, he lost three generations. He lost his mom. He lost his wife. He lost his young daughter. He himself somehow walked away without physical injury. In this radio interview, he talked about what it was like to experience such a major loss. Eventually he wrote a book called *A Grace Disguised* in which he describes going through this difficult journey. And here is what he concluded:

> The experience of loss does not need to be the defining moment of our story.

He went on to say that the defining moment can be *our response* to the loss. Ultimately our story doesn't have to be a story about loss; it can be a story about how we respond to the loss.

When difficult circumstances come your way, when there is a famine in the land, how will you respond? If you let Him, God will use those circumstances to wake you up and ultimately draw you closer to Him.

Deserved Consequences

Sometimes God gets our attention through difficult circumstances, but more often God brings us to a desperate moment through deserved consequences.

In the parable of the prodigal son, Jesus pointed out that the son spent all his money on wild living. That was no one else's fault. The son arrived in the distant country; he lived it up for a time; and after many nights of buying rounds and throwing parties, he was left with an empty wine glass *and* an empty wallet. The money was gone, and there was no one to blame but himself. His own actions and choices brought about consequences.

He found himself in a pigpen, so hungry he longed to fill his stomach with pig slop. If he hadn't left his father's house and hadn't blown all his money on wild living, he wouldn't have found himself in this position.

The consequences of our choices can be a jarring alarm that wakes us up and causes us to come to our senses. When you are in the Distant Country, it's only a matter of time before your decisions catch up to you. That desperate moment is the time to cry out to God.

A few months ago, I was speaking at a church in Las Vegas. It was Sunday morning, and I was driving to the church when I got pulled over for "drunk driving." There is a reason I put those words in quotes. I wasn't drunk. However, I had made some poor choices that led up to this moment.

Poor Choice #1: When I got off the plane and headed to the car-rental counter, I decided I was going to try to charm my way into getting upgraded to a convertible—which turned out to be pretty easy. It was 114 degrees outside, and every single convertible they had was available. So I was driving in a canary-yellow Mustang convertible with the top down early on a Sunday morning.

Poor Choice #2: I wasn't supposed to be staying on the Strip, but because I wanted to be close to the action, I got a room at the Holiday Inn right behind a casino. So it looked like I was pulling out of a casino, driving a convertible with its top down early on Sunday morning.

Poor Choice #3: I was running a little bit late that morning, so I left my room looking a little disheveled. I say a *little* disheveled, but honestly, I looked like a mess with my shirt untucked, my hair gloriously, bed-headedly askew, and my pants more wrinkled than normal. At the time, I didn't think much of it. I figured I'd be able to touch up my hair and make myself look presentable after I arrived at the church. So it looked like I was pulling out of a casino, driving a convertible early on a Sunday morning, and I happened to look like the victim of an all-night bender.

Poor Choice #4: I had run into a gas station the night before to get some gum and made a last-minute decision to splurge on IBC Root Beer. I love IBC Root Beer, but my wife's not a big fan because it's more expensive since it comes in a glass bottle. A little was left over, and I decided to finish off the bottle as I drove with messed-up hair and wrinkled clothes out of a casino in a convertible with its top down early on Sunday morning.

Poor Choice #5: When the police officer pulled me over for drunk driving, the situation struck me not just as humorous, but as hilarious. I started laughing and couldn't stop, which I am known to do in completely inappropriate situations.[3] This frustrated the officer, who explained to me that this was not a laughing matter. As I tried to stop laughing, I explained to him that I wasn't drunk but on my way to go preach at a church.

To which he responded, "That's exactly what a drunk person would say."

As he walked back to his car, my laughter devolved into soft chuckling.

When he got back into his car, I was only smiling.

Once he got on the radio with my license in hand, I started waking up to reality.

I retraced my steps, and my five poor choices became evident. I suddenly got this sick feeling in my stomach—the emotional equivalent of eating a bean burrito in less than ninety seconds. I realized that all of this had gone horribly wrong, and it could get much worse. So while I was waiting for the police officer in my canary-yellow convertible, do you know what I started doing? I prayed—and with great fervor, I might add.

---

3   For example: When my wife was pregnant with our first child and we went to the hospital for birthing classes, they showed us a video of women in labor. I couldn't stop laughing. My wife failed to see the humor.

Sometimes we don't see the poor choices we are making in the moment, but the weight of possible consequences can help us look back upon our poor choices with greater clarity. And the moment the consequences of our decisions catch up to us is an invitation to cry out to God for help.

The prophet Jonah experienced this moment after God gave him an assignment to go preach against sin in the great city of Nineveh.

You have to understand that Nineveh was not what you might call a tourist hot spot. It was a powerful city in Assyria. The Assyrians were a feared world power known for their cruelty. They didn't just conquer a nation; they practiced genocide and were known for torturing enemies. The Old Testament prophet Nahum spoke of the city of Nineveh and said:

> Woe to the city of blood, full of lies, full of plunder, never without victims!… piles of dead, bodies without number, people stumbling over the corpses. (Nah. 3:1–3)

You get the picture.

This was the last place Jonah wanted to go, so he decided to take a boat in the opposite direction. Nineveh was about 600 miles northeast, but instead, Jonah set out for a city called Tarshish, which was 2,000 miles in the opposite direction. Quite literally, Jonah ran away from God and headed to the distant country.

Jonah was on the ship heading to Tarshish when God sent a violent storm. When I'm on a boat, any storm is a bad storm. But a storm sent by God? This was the kind of storm that tossed the boat around like a toy in a bathtub. The ship's beams groaned from the violent waves, threatening to break apart. Scripture says the sailors were terrified. This is a bad sign. When the salty seafarers are quaking in their boots, you know things are *bad*. The sailors cried out to their gods and gave up any hope of overcoming the storm themselves. That's like the captain of an airplane getting on the intercom and saying, "This weather's really bad, folks. I've lost control of the plane, and I'm really scared right now. Would everybody please start praying? By the way, I'm about to open the cargo hold and let all our luggage plummet to the ground."

That's what the captain of Jonah's ship did.

While the crew threw out all the ship's cargo, the captain told everyone aboard to pray, and then he found Jonah belowdecks. Amazingly, Jonah was asleep in the bottom of the boat! When the pagan captain found Jonah sleeping in the hull, he shook him awake and said, "How can you sleep? Get up and call on your god! Maybe he will take notice of us so that we will not perish."

And this is where some of you find yourself. You are sleeping through the storm. Everyone around you can see it, but you are dozing off in the midst of impending disaster. You need someone to wake you up.

As a pastor, this is a role with which I'm familiar. Many times I've had to run belowdecks, find someone who was sleeping through a storm in their life, and wake the person up. So let me play the part of this captain for a moment, because you may be reading this and desperately be needing to wake up and call upon God.

To the husband whose marriage is falling apart but who seems indifferent and too distracted by video games or golf to fight for his wife. *Wake up!*

To the college student who has developed a habit of getting drunk and sleeping with strangers. *Wake up!*

To the mother who yells at her kids and doesn't remember the last time she really knelt beside their bed to pray for them. *Wake up!*

To the father who leaves for work before his kids get up and gets home after they're in bed for the night. *Wake up!*

Come to your senses! There is a storm brewing, and there is no time to waste. Don't fool yourself into thinking that those closest to you will be able to escape the devastation of your storm. Your journey to the Distant Country doesn't affect just you, but all those who share their life with you.

When Jonah ran from God, the sailors were terrified and began throwing their possessions overboard. His running from God destroyed the lives of the people around him.

So it's not just me yelling at you to wake up.

It's a friend, a spouse, a parent yelling, "Wake up!"

It's the voice of a child saying, "Mom, wake up!" or "Dad, wake up!"

Desperation Reveals Dependence

Oftentimes, our desperate moments reveal our inherent dependence on the Father. It was always true; it just took a moment of desperation for us to come to our senses and realize it. The son's desperation after running out of money and having a famine force him into a pigpen revealed that he'd been dependent upon his father his whole life—*and still was.*

Think about it: he grew up in his father's house; he ate food from his father's fields; he was sustained by his father's provision and clothed with his father's coin; and he refreshed himself with water from his father's well. In order to make his break from his father, where did he turn for the funding? *His father!* He went to the man he wanted to leave to ask for money so he could afford to do so. Even in his rebellion, he was dependent on the father! He lived off his inheritance from the father as he traveled to the Distant Country and partied like each day was the last of his life, and it was only when he ran out of his father's money that he became desperate.

Here's my question: How desperate will your situation become before you realize your dependence? Eventually, the money will run out and famine will come.

The boss calls you in, sits you down, and says, "I'm sorry; we're downsizing."

The bank sends a letter marked *foreclosure*.

The landlord posts an eviction notice on your door.

The creditors call, asking about the bills you've yet to pay.

The tests come back with a diagnosis of cancer.

The phone rings; there has been an accident.

There will be a desperate moment, a difficult circumstance, maybe a deserved consequence, when you will realize that your way isn't working and you need your heavenly Father.

What's It Going to Take?

On occasion I speak to a group of inmates at the Kentucky State Penitentiary. They file into the room, one after the other. There's not much pretense or pride. They're all dressed alike. It's hard to get caught up in impressing people when everyone wears the same outfit—an outfit that declares they are guilty.

The inmates could teach the church a lot about authenticity and transparency. Last time I was there, I talked about the Prodigal Son and how he had this moment of awakening when he came to his senses. Afterward, one of the inmates came up to me and showed me a picture of his family, his wife and two young kids, that he kept in his Bible. As he looked at it, his eyes welled with tears, and he said to me, "I tried it my way for a long time, and it didn't work, so now I'm doing things His way." I put my arm around the inmate and told him I was proud of him. But as he stared at his picture, he added, "I just wish it hadn't taken being sent here for me to come to my senses."

Over the years I've noticed something people often say after they come to their senses and return home from the Distant Country. They say, "Well, I had to hit rock bottom." Have you ever heard that? I don't know why we tell ourselves we have to hit rock bottom. I suppose it makes us feel better about how far we fell.

Listen to me, I don't know what it's going to take, but I know you don't have to hit rock bottom. You can wake up now. You can come to your senses today.

Chapter 4

A STARTLING
REALIZATION

In the mid-90s this type of artwork that, if you looked at it just right, you could see a hidden picture, became popular. Do you remember those? You'd stare and stare and then suddenly a 3-D image appeared. Did you like them? I hated them! I could never see the image.

A neighborhood friend named Terry Good had one hanging on his wall, and whenever I would go over to his house, I'd stare at that piece of artwork until I felt like my eyes were bleeding. He would stand next to me and say, "Do you see it? How about now? Do you see it now?"

And I would reply, "See what? I don't see anything."

Then he would say something like, "You have to really *want* to see it."

Well, what was I supposed to do? I was staring a hole through the artwork, and I still didn't see anything. He tried to help with an additional piece of advice: "Whatever you do, don't blink." Have you ever tried not to blink? The harder you try not to blink, the more likely it is that it will happen. Seriously. Put this book down right now, stare at something, and repeatedly tell yourself not to blink. Eventually I decided the hidden 3-D picture was either a practical joke or Terry was smoking something.

Then one day, after fighting the instinct to blink for twenty-seven minutes, I suddenly saw it! It was a sailboat floating among the clouds. Do you know what my response was? Massive disappointment.

But here's the point: for a long time I was staring at the picture right in front of me, and I couldn't see it. Then suddenly I saw it.

Have you had that kind of sudden awakening? You finally saw something that was right in front of you? The Prodigal Son came to his senses when he was sitting in the pigpen so hungry that he longed to fill his stomach with the pig slop when he suddenly realized it didn't have to be like this.

In Luke 15:17, we read his startling realization:

> How many of my father's hired servants have food
> to spare, and here I am starving to death!

Have you ever had a moment like this? The Holy Spirit opens your eyes, and you see something that you had somehow missed before. You have a startling realization that changes everything.

A while back, a wife told me her and her husband's AHA story:

> My husband and I both had an AHA moment
> about two years ago when we suddenly realized we
> were living as fans of Christ instead of as completely

committed followers. We discovered that Jesus wanted us to totally surrender all that we are to Him. We decided then to totally surrender our lives to God. Soon after that we felt led to adopt a little girl from Ethiopia. We didn't know at the time that God's plan was actually for us to adopt a sibling group of three children! Our lives have never been crazier, but neither have we ever felt more joy or fulfillment!

One father told me about praying for his daughter for seven years—her whole life—that God would use her in a powerful way. At the same time, for the past three years, he had also been asking God to heal her from life-threatening cancer. Her illness had given her opportunities to tell many doctors and nurses about her faith in Jesus. Several of her extended family members had started coming to church as a direct result of seeing the supernatural strength with which she battled her illness. One night the father prayed the same prayer he had prayed her whole life—that God would use her powerfully—but when he prayed that God would heal her completely, he came to such a startling realization it was like he could almost hear God asking him, "Well, which one do you want? You have prayed her entire life for her to be an awesome witness, and now she is."

Jesus put it this way: the truth will set you free.

Have you had some moments like this? Moments when you realized something you never had before?

You realize you've been trying to living out the Christian life from your own power and strength rather than out of the power of the Holy Spirit.

You realize you weren't actually following Jesus; you were just following a list of rules and rituals.

You realize the reason you struggle with food is that you are trying to satisfy your soul by filling your stomach.

You realize you've put incredible pressure on your romantic relationship, because you've been looking to your significant other to do for you what only God can do for you.

You realize you are stressed out about money, because you're putting your trust in money instead of in God.

You realize you spent so much of your life wrestling with guilt and shame, because you thought being good enough would save you instead of relying on the grace of God to save you.

Suddenly you realize a truth.

That truth has always been true, but for some reason, you just didn't see it before. Like the Prodigal Son, it was the right time and the right place, and finally a startling realization woke you up and brought you to your senses.

Silence and Solitude

For the Prodigal Son to finally make this startling realization, he had to have some time alone. Some time to think. Maybe this was the first time in a long time that he'd sat in silence. Even now, though, it wasn't his choice. He'd run out of money, his friends had bailed on him, a famine swept over the land, and he was driven to the pigpen. There was no one to talk to in the pigpen. There was nothing to distract him. He was alone in the Distant Country, forced away from the noise of wild living and parties. No more staying up into the early hours of morning and sleeping in late with no time for sober thinking and reflection.

If you're in need of a startling realization in your life, begin with solitude and silence. You may find that God has been trying to get your attention for a while but you haven't been able to hear Him. Not because He hasn't been loud enough, but because you haven't been quiet enough.

Imagine you're at home watching a game. You have the TV turned up fairly loud, but someone is using the blender in the kitchen, someone else is running the vacuum cleaner in the living room, and one of the kids has their radio cranked up down the hallway. You think, *I just need to turn up the volume.* So you grab the remote to turn the television volume even louder only to find that it's already turned all the way up. But you still can't hear the game.

What's the problem? The problem isn't the volume. The problem is that you need to turn down the interfering noises.

When God speaks to us, He often speaks in moments of solitude and silence. One of the prophet Elijah's AHA moments with God took place on a mountain. Elijah went to the mountain to meet with God, but when he got there, God hadn't yet appeared. While Elijah waited, there was a strong wind blowing through the area, and Elijah thought, *Oh, God must be in that wind.*

However, the wind died down, and God wasn't in the wind. Then there was an earthquake that shook the whole mountain, and Elijah thought, *God's in the earthquake.* But God wasn't in the earthquake. And then there was a fire that swept through the area and Elijah thought, *Well, God must be in the fire.* But the fire subsided, and God wasn't in the fire.

Those are ways we would expect God to speak to us.

But the Bible tells us that God spoke to Elijah in a gentle whisper. The literal translation here speaks of a sound that is even quieter than a whisper. The NRSV translates it as "a sound of sheer silence" (1 Kings 19:12). That's when Elijah heard from the Lord.

For many of us, a little silence and solitude are the only things standing between us and a startling realization. But silence and solitude don't seem to be in our nature. When we find our lives falling apart in the Distant Country, we get desperate, and we want to make it happen ourselves.

A number of years ago, my youngest daughter was in the backyard trying to catch butterflies. At this time of year, we had a bunch of butterflies staying in a certain area of our farm. From inside the house, I watched as she tried to grab a butterfly. She wanted one so badly she was working up a sweat thrashing around trying to grab hold of one. She wasn't trying to catch one so much as she was trying to *seize* one. Her arms flew around as she lunged toward one butterfly, then another. After watching her for a few minutes, I realized that the more frustrated she became, the more aggressive and forceful she was.

I finally went outside and explained how to catch a butterfly.

"Look," I said, "I know what I'm about to ask you is going to be really hard, but if you want to catch a butterfly, you need to be still and quiet. If you can just stand in the middle of them and be still and quiet, after a few moments, one of them will land on you."

She looked skeptical but was desperate enough to give it a shot. As I watched from a distance, she waited for one to land on her, and sure enough, after a few moments, one landed on her knee. And the moment that poor butterfly landed on her knee, she grabbed it.

Sometimes we want to seize AHA, but AHA is not often seized; it is received. Often, against all human intuition, that simply requires a little silence and solitude.

Do you have some quiet moments set aside in the busy-ness of your life? The Bible says in Psalms to "Be still." God says, "Be still and know that I am God" (Ps. 46:10). I like this definition of stillness: silence on the outside and surrender on the inside.

Recently, I read about a church in England that recorded the "sound of silence" on a CD and provided the CD to the congregation with the challenge to listen to it once a day over the next week. It was marketed as a half-hour of listening to absolutely nothing. What's crazy is that this church has been selling the CD to customers around the world.

You may not have a recording of the sound of silence readily available, but I would encourage you to get alone with your Bible and spend some time in solitude and silence anyway.

AHA often begins in the stillness.

Flip the Switch

A few months ago, a handyman came to our house to hang a light fixture in the kitchen, because I was having a busy week. Well, that and the fact that I'm the least handy man you will ever meet.[1] When the handyman came over, he got everything hooked up.

---

1 True story: Growing up my dad taught me the only two tools needed to fix anything are a telephone and checkbook. His toolbox consisted of a hammer and Super Glue.

He connected all the appropriate wires and then flipped the light switch. Nothing happened.

I admit that I was secretly delighted with his failure.

He rewired it and turned it on again, but it still didn't work. He took everything down, disconnected the wires, and started over. But it still didn't work.

My wife was watching this, and she was starting to get a little frustrated, thinking the fixture she bought from the store was a dud. Meanwhile, I'd analyzed the situation[2] and had become fairly certain that he wasn't flipping the right switch. He was flipping the one next to the one I thought he should be flipping. But I wasn't going to say anything about my hypothesis out of fear of being wrong and eliciting further mockery and humiliation for my lack of skills.

Eventually, I waited until he had it hooked up again and walked over to the wall to flip the correct switch. Immediately the light came on. *How do you like me now, Mr. Handyman?* It was right there in front of him; he just needed someone else to flip the switch.

Sometimes in our life, the startling realization only takes place when someone else steps in with a healthy perspective and flips the switch for us. For the Prodigal Son, and for many of us, what would really help is a little solitude and silence, but sometimes we also need someone in our lives to tell us the truth.

In 2 Kings 5, we read about an army commander in desperate need of someone to flip the switch.

---

2   Honestly, I'm never too busy to analyze the failings of a man who is supposed to be handier than me.

Naaman was a successful and highly regarded military official for the king of Aram, and in the Bible he's described as a brave warrior. But Naaman's life started to fall apart when he was afflicted with a horrible skin disease.

After a few raids on Israel, Naaman brought home a young Israelite girl to serve his wife. This Israelite girl spoke to her mistress, saying, "If only my master could meet the prophet of Samaria, he would be healed of his skin disease."

When Naaman's wife told him this, he got the king's blessing to go and meet this prophet, named Elisha. The king of Aram even sent a letter with Naaman to the king of Israel, a kind of intimidation tactic that read: "When you get this letter, you'll know that I've personally sent my servant Naaman to you; heal him of his skin disease."

Translation: "You better fix this guy—or else."

The king of Israel got the letter and panicked. Who wouldn't? He tore his clothes in anguish, crying out, "Am I a god with the power to bring death or life that I get orders to heal this man from his disease?" To be fair to the king of Israel, this was a particularly unfair situation. The king of Aram was using this situation to create yet another excuse to raid Israel and make war against God's people.

Then the prophet Elisha heard of the king's anguish, and he told the king not to worry, asking him to send Naaman to him. So Naaman made his way to the prophet he'd heard so much about, all in the hopes of being healed.

And Scripture says that Naaman was not traveling lightly. We read that he had with him "750 pounds of silver, 150 pounds of gold, and ten sets of clothes" (2 Kings 5:5 MSG). So Naaman arrived at the prophet's house with his entourage, including horses and chariots, clothes and supplies. Clearly, Naaman had come prepared to earn his healing, no matter what the prophet would order. A quest to the edge of Israel? Bring it on. A specific mountain he would need to climb or a people that needed conquering? No problem. Naaman was ready for whatever the prophet would throw at him—except, of course, Elisha's curveball response.

Second Kings 5:10 says, "Elisha sent out a servant to meet him with this message: 'Go to the River Jordan and immerse yourself seven times. Your skin will be healed and you'll be as good as new'" (MSG).

Seems like a simple enough request, right?

However, Elisha had insulted Naaman in every way possible with this message. Naaman arrived at Elisha's door with his caravan, and the prophet didn't even come outside to greet him. Instead, Elisha sent a messenger. Naaman was not the kind of guy who received messengers. He *sent* messengers.

In response to the message, Naaman stormed off in a huff. In his anger, he began to complain, saying, "I thought he'd personally come out and meet me, call on the name of God, wave his hand over the diseased spot, and get rid of the disease."

Naaman had pictured this going down a certain way. He'd expected the prophet to display some pomp and circumstance. On top of that, Naaman was not going to debase himself in an Israeli river. He continued complaining, saying, "The Damascus rivers, Abana and Pharpar, are cleaner by far than any of the rivers in Israel. Why not bathe in them? I'd at least get clean" (2 Kings 5:11–12 MSG).

Naaman sulked, in desperate need of an AHA. Unless he had a startling realization, he wouldn't be healed. He needed someone to flip the switch, but who would it be? Elisha, the prophet and man of God? No. Perhaps a fellow soldier in the caravan? No. Of all the people, it was a servant.

A servant approached the sulking commander, and here's what he said: "Father, if the prophet had asked you to do something hard and heroic, wouldn't you have done it? So why not this simple 'wash and be clean'?" (2 Kings 5:13 MSG).

The servant pointed out a simple truth. Naaman came ready for an epic adventure or a grand healing ceremony. He came prepared to pay any price for his healing. So why not just wash? In the nicest way possible, this servant said, "Get over yourself and take a bath."

Naaman heard these words and experienced a startling realization. Immediately, Naaman went down to the Jordan and washed seven times. God cleansed him of his disease, and he returned to Elisha to articulate his awakening. In verse 15, Naaman declared, "I now know beyond a shadow of a doubt that there is no God anywhere on earth other than the God of Israel."

AHA.

My question is: Do you have someone in your life who can flip a switch if it's needed? Often we are the last ones to see the hard truth in our own lives. It's right in front of us, but somehow we miss it.

Do you have a friend like that? Have you given someone permission and freedom to speak the truth to you even when it's not easy?

We have a tendency in our relationships—even our closest ones—to speak 95 percent of the truth. We don't take it the full 100 percent. But that last 5 percent is what really needs to be said. More often than not, the startling realization takes place in the 5 percent of hard truth. All of us need a relationship with someone who has permission to flip the switch we missed.

I recently read an article in the *Montreal Gazette* about a man named Pierre-Paul Thomas. He was born blind and could only imagine the world that was often described to him. For years he walked with a white cane to avoid obstacles in front of him. But at the age of sixty-six, Thomas fell down the stairs in an apartment building and fractured the bones of his face. He was rushed to the hospital with severe swelling around his eyes. A team of doctors went to work to repair the bones. Months later he went to be examined by a plastic surgeon for a consultation about repairing his scalp. The surgeon casually asked Thomas, "Oh, while we're at it, do you want us to fix your eyes, too?"

Thomas did not understand. Nor did he know how to respond.

Not long after that, Thomas had surgery and could truly see for the first time. Suddenly his world consisted of bright colors he had never fathomed before. He spoke of being awestruck by flowers blossoming and trees blooming.

As beautiful as this story of a sixty-six-year-old man who was able to see for the first time is, there is a sad reality. He could have had the same surgery at a younger age and been able to see earlier. Thomas had assumed such a possibility was impossible and had resigned himself to a life of blindness when, in reality, he could have experienced the gift of sight decades earlier.[3]

---

3   Aaron Derfel, "Blind No More: 'It's like I'm a Child All Over Again," *Montreal Gazette*, July 26, 2013, http://www.montrealgazette.com/health/Blind+more +like+child+over+again+video/8711875/story.html.

I don't want to spend any part of my life missing out on what God wants me to see now. I don't want to come to my senses in twenty years if God is trying to wake me up now.

It may be a desperate moment or a startling realization, but I can't help but wonder if God is trying to get your attention.

Lord, open our eyes that we may see.

PART 2
BRUTAL HONESTY

He said to himself ...

Chapter 5

TALKING TO YOURSELF

A number of years ago, I was getting my hair cut at the barbershop.[1] I was sitting in the chair, and I couldn't help but notice that the lady cutting my hair kept looking at me in the mirror in front of us. I didn't think much of it initially, but then I couldn't help but notice as her staring got more intense. Finally she stopped cutting my hair altogether and just stared. Now I was looking at myself in the mirror as well, trying to figure out the problem. I thought maybe she'd cut my hair a little too short on one side and was trying to figure out how to balance it on the other. I gave my hair a once-over, and it seemed fine. The lady, though, was still staring at my reflection in the mirror with an expression on her face that said, "There's something wrong with you."

But then she noticed that I was staring at her staring at me, and her expression changed slightly. She raised her eyebrows with a look

---

1 I don't know why, but as a man, I feel weird calling it a salon. Maybe that's what it says on the sign, but I was getting my hair cut at a barbershop.

that said, "Are you seeing what I'm seeing?" At this point, I was afraid to ask, so we both went back to looking at my reflection in the mirror.

We did this for a few more seconds, and then, without warning, she pulled on my right ear and asked, "Don't you see it?" But I didn't see it, so she tugged harder on my ear, expecting me to recognize whatever it was she had discovered. I was still oblivious. Finally she dropped the bomb: "Did you realize your right ear sticks out farther from your head than your left ear?"

And now we were both looking at it. Things seemed to be moving in slow motion.

Oh. My. Goodness, I thought. *She's right. I've woken up every morning and looked at myself in the mirror for thirty-plus years and never noticed it, but this complete stranger cutting my hair is spot-on. My right ear sticks out farther from my head than my left ear. How have I not seen this before?*

I was in a cold sweat and tried to jolt out of the state of shock I was in. She was still staring, almost measuring just how far the ear protruded. Not knowing how to respond but compelled to say something, I asked, "Well, is there ... is there anything you can do about it—you know, to fix it?"

I was hoping she brought this up because she had a solution. Maybe she could make a couple of adjustments to my typical haircut, maybe layer a little differently on each side so it would balance out. Instead, she said, "No, I think it's just one of those things you have to learn to live with."

Well, thanks, barbershop lady. Thanks a million. You've now told me something I can never unknow. Now when I wake up each morning, I'm going to look in the mirror and see that Dumbo ear sticking out and ask,

"Why me?" And I'll fall asleep right-side down in hopes my mutant ear will crease a little during the night, and for a few hours in the morning, at least, I can be normal—until it flops back out.

Honest Look in the Mirror

Have you ever learned something about yourself or had someone tell you something, and it completely changed things for you? You were awakened to some truth, and from then on, you could never unlearn or unhear it? AHA entails more than just an awakening; it requires honesty.

One of my favorite preachers of all time is a man named Fred Craddock. He is in his eighties now but is widely regarded as one of the most effective communicators of God's Word in the past century. I recently read an article about him on CNN's website entitled "A Preaching 'Genius' Faces His Toughest Convert."

The story was about Fred Craddock's father, Fred Craddock Sr. He was not a Christian and was often skeptical of faith and critical of the church. Other preachers who lived near his father would try to reach out to Fred's dad.

"I know what the church wants," Fred Sr. would say. "Another name; another pledge." His father was convinced that the church just wanted another name for its membership and another dollar for its offering.

As his father grew older, he began to have more serious health problems. One day Fred's mother called and said, "You need to go see your father. He may not live much longer." So Craddock visited his father in a VA hospital in Memphis, Tennessee. He had wasted away to seventy-three pounds. Radiation treatments had destroyed him. He couldn't eat. He couldn't speak.

Craddock learned that even though his dad wasn't a part of the church, a local church had faithfully visited his father. People had come to visit him and pray with him. People from the church had brought meals over to the house and sent cards and flowers. And slowly the heart of his father had softened.

One day when Fred was sitting with his father in the hospital, his father reached over and picked up a Kleenex box next to his bed. He grabbed a pen and jotted something down. Fred leaned in to read the words from Shakespeare's *Hamlet*: "In this harsh world, draw your breath in pain to tell my story."

"What's your story, Daddy?" Fred asked.

His father's eyes filled with tears.

He wrote three brutally honest words: "I was wrong."[2]

There was a sudden awakening that led to brutal honesty.

But many of us never get past the awakening. If we can't bring ourselves to honestly say, "I was wrong," AHA won't happen.

Talking to Myself

In Luke 15, we see the second ingredient of AHA: Brutal Honesty. In the New Living Translation, after the Prodigal Son came to his senses, verse 17 reads:

---

2   John Blake, "A Preaching 'Genius' Faces His Toughest Convert," *CNN*, December 14, 2011, http://www.cnn.com/2011/11/27/us/craddock-profile/index.html.

He said to himself …

There was no one else around. It was just him and the pigs. Sometimes the hardest conversation to have is the one you have with yourself. Brutal honesty begins when we look in the mirror and speak the truth about what we see. AHA requires you to tell the truth about yourself *to* yourself. The Prodigal Son said to himself,

> How many of my father's hired servants have food to spare, and here I am starving to death! I will set out and go back to my father and say to him: Father, I have sinned against heaven and against you. I am no longer worthy to be called your son; make me like one of your hired servants. (Luke 15:17–19)

He was honest with himself about what he deserved. That kind of honesty is difficult. The hardest person in the world to be honest with is the person in the mirror, and I don't mean the lady who's cutting your hair—I mean *you*. We'd prefer the awakening without the brutal honesty.

Like the wife who wakes up to her critical spirit but refuses to say, "I have been wrong to be so negative. I know my husband needs my encouragement and support, but I've just complained and criticized."

Like the husband who realizes his sexual sin but refuses to say, "My pornography problem has created a wedge in my marriage and has hardened my heart toward my wife."

No one wants to say those things. No one wants to look in the mirror and admit:

I have chosen to sit on a couch watching SportsCenter over being a spiritual leader in my home.

I go shopping and spend money we don't have to make me feel better about the things in my life that I can't control.

I haven't had real faith in years. I'm pretending to be someone I'm not to impress the people around me, but the truth is I'm a hypocrite.

Avoiding brutal honesty will short-circuit lasting change. When there is recognition without repentance, AHA doesn't happen. When the Prodigal Son came to his senses, he dealt with himself truthfully. The awakening must lead to honesty. Conviction must lead to confession.

This is the biggest difference between regret and repentance. Many of us will have an awakening and regret that things have turned out the way they have, but we won't repent of our part in it. We regret that someone has noticed and pointed out our wrongs, but we'd rather continue to deceive them and prove ourselves right than actually confess the truth.

Over the last number of years, we've seen regular public confessions from politicians, sports figures, and business leaders. The order of events is predictable. The public figure is caught and then exposed. We read the scandalous story in the news. The next day or two, the public figure issues an official apology and typically commits to getting some kind of professional help.

Susan Wise Bauer wrote a book about such apologies. In the book, called *The Art of the Public Grovel*, she makes a helpful distinction between an apology and a confession: "An apology is an expression of regret: *I am sorry.* A confession is an admission of fault: *I am sorry because I did wrong. I sinned.*"[3]

As a pastor it is not unusual for me to talk to someone who comes to confess a sin or some kind of ongoing struggle. When I sit down with that person, there are often tears as they admit the truth. I know it's a difficult and humbling thing to do, because I have been in that seat many times. But one of the questions I've learned to ask is, "Are you confessing this to me because you got caught?"

This is almost always the case.

Her husband found the email correspondence, and the emotional affair was undeniable.

His parents found a joint in the floorboard of the car.

His boss finally fired him for coming to work drunk.

She couldn't pay her credit card bills and a court case was brewing.

His college grades were finally posted and partying had obviously taken its toll.

Her pregnancy test came back positive, and she wasn't sure who the father was.

His daughter walked in and saw what he was looking at on the computer.

More often than not, the confessions I hear are motivated by discovery. Just because they were caught doesn't mean the honesty

---

3   Susan Wise Bauer, *The Art of the Public Grovel* (Princeton: Princeton University Press, 2008), 2.

isn't sincere, but it makes it more difficult to know if I'm listening to regret or repentance.

If you're a parent, chances are you've seen this in your children. If you catch your child with his hand in the proverbial cookie jar—or the literal cookie jar—the child may say, "I'm sorry." But is the apology honest? Is the child sorry for getting a cookie without permission, or is the child sorry for getting caught? Usually the child is just sorry he didn't have a better plan to heist the cookies.

Hebrews 4:13 reads:

> Nothing in all creation is hidden from God's sight.
> Everything is uncovered and laid bare before the
> eyes of him to whom we must give account.

Our heavenly Father sees and knows all, so it's not a question of getting caught. The honesty I'm talking about is more than a simple acknowledgment; it is a kind of brokenness. Yes, you tell the person who caught you that you are sorry, but you must go beyond that. In an honest moment when no one else is around, you must tell yourself the truth about yourself and know that you are sorry.

That's the difference between regret and repentance.

So here's the question: Have you followed up an awakening by being brutally honest with yourself?

If you're reading this at home, here's what I want you to do: Get up and go to a bathroom. Shut the door behind you. One at a time, read these questions out loud. After each question, look at yourself in the mirror and speak the honest truth. Some of these won't apply to you, but I hope they will move you to ask yourself some relevant, hard questions.

1. Did you spend more time this week on Facebook or in prayer?

2. When was the last time you told someone, "I love you"?

3. How specifically have you helped someone in need in the last month?

4. When was the last time you said to someone, "I was wrong. Please forgive me"?

5. What's on your DVR at home? Your computer's history?

6. When was the last time you prayed with your spouse? With your children?

7. Can you name one missionary whom you pray for?

8. What sin have you not confessed to God or anyone else?

9. When was the last time you sat with an open Bible?

10. Did you spend more money this month eating out than on advancing the kingdom of God?

11. When was the last time you cried over your sin?

12. Who besides God knows about your secret sin?

So let me guess: you just scanned through the questions and didn't take the time to actually do the above exercise.

How do I know that about you? Because I know what I would do if I were reading this book. I would read through the challenge and think to myself, *I get it. I understand the point the author is trying to make. What an insightful guy.* Or something like that. Then I would move on, letting myself off the hook once again.

Listen, I hope you will actually do the challenge.

I'll even create the section break right here so you don't feel pressured to read on. There is something powerful about going into a quiet room, shutting the door, looking in the mirror, and speaking truth *to yourself* about yourself.

Honest with Others

I'll tell you up front that you aren't going to like this next part. You'll probably think of some reasons why this next piece isn't really pertinent to your situation and why it doesn't apply to you. You'll probably try to find a way around it by choosing to hear this as more of a helpful hint than a nonnegotiable. But I'm telling you—AHA won't happen without it.

Brutal honesty begins with telling yourself the truth about yourself, which is difficult, but the next step is even harder. You must tell the truth about yourself to someone else.

The Prodigal Son understood that there was no way around it. After telling the truth to himself about his situation and what he deserved, he realized he also needed to be honest with his father. In Luke 15:18, he says:

> I will set out and go back to my father and say
> to him: Father, I have sinned against heaven and
> against you.

He recognized that it wasn't enough for him to be honest with himself; he also needed to be honest with his father. Most of us don't practice voluntary confession. Not when it comes to being honest with ourselves, but especially not when it comes to confessing to others. Voluntary confession is when we regularly and voluntarily acknowledge our sin and honestly admit our weaknesses to someone in our lives. To some of us, it may seem like an act of self-sabotage.

Imagine you're speeding, going eighty miles per hour in a sixty-five-mile-per-hour zone. You look down and realize how fast you are going and slow down. There is an awakening, and you are honest with yourself. Surely that is enough. But imagine you see a police officer the next day, and you go up to him and say, "Officer, I want you to know that yesterday I was going eighty miles per hour in a sixty-five-mile-per-hour zone." That never happens. We don't voluntarily confess cheating on a test, getting high, flirting with a coworker, or losing our temper. Instead, we tend to confess only when the evidence indicts us.

It's especially true for Christians. If you're a Christian, you know there are certain things that should not be a part of your life. If you weren't a Christian, confessing or acknowledging those things wouldn't be a big deal. You'd just go to the local sports bar, knock back a couple of beers, and say with great pride, "I like pornography." And some of the regulars might even raise their glasses in agreement. But when we as Christians find ourselves struggling, our instinct is to hide those things instead of confess them.

I would say that's excruciatingly true for pastors. Throughout my time as a minister, I have felt a pressure to maintain a certain image. People perceive me to be spiritual and holy, and I find myself wanting to pretend to be more than I really am. And I know that when I confess my sin to others, the words often get stuck in my throat, and I start to justify all the reasons it would be better to be seen and respected as someone who's got it all figured out. But the problem is, I don't have it all figured out. Not even close. I've learned the hard way that unless I'm willing to be brutally honest with someone else, the AHA process stalls.

Let me just acknowledge something for a second: some of you are reading this and thinking, *No way am I going to tell anyone else about my secrets. It would be humiliating to share my mistakes.*

I know how you feel. I know how sick to my stomach I feel when I even think about telling someone I'm wrestling with something. It's embarrassing. It makes me feel like a stupid kid who doesn't know what to do. When you're going the wrong way, it's hard enough to admit it to yourself, but the last thing you want is to have someone else find out you're lost. But consider the alternative for a second. When we don't share these struggles with someone, what options do we have? Pretend we know where we're headed? That's never worked out well—at least, not for me.

Men, have you ever been on a road trip when your wife tells you you're going the wrong way? My wife has an annoyingly accurate sense of direction, so this is a familiar scenario for me.

I remember one occasion in particular. It was our first year of marriage, and we were returning from a vacation in Branson. I took the back roads, because I'm a man, and there are few things I enjoy more than taking shortcuts.

As we drove, my wife said to me, "This isn't the right direction."

I dismissed it the first time, but when she repeated her concern, I got defensive. She kept commenting, and I kept driving. I kept cutting down wooded roads, annoyed that my wife would have any doubts about my ability to get us home. But—and I've never actually told her this—after one too many turns, I realized she was right and I was lost. I drove around confidently, not wanting her to know that inside I was praying I would see a mailbox, a tractor, anything that looked familiar.

By this point, I'd had the awakening, but I refused to acknowledge the reality of the situation. Here is the strategy that I came up with—just spur-of-the-moment male brilliance. I thought to myself, *I'm going to wait until she falls asleep. Then I'll turn this car around.*

And that's exactly what I did.

I intentionally drove the wrong direction for another twenty minutes, waiting for her to fall asleep. When she finally nodded off, I turned the car around and sped home. When I pulled into the driveway, I woke her up and said, "See, honey. We're home. I told you I knew where I was going."

Am I the only one who does that? The only one who realizes I'm going the wrong direction, have the awakening, have the sudden recognition—but instead of being honest about it, just say, "I'm just going to keep going."

Honesty that Brings Healing

In the first part of this chapter, the challenge was to be honest with yourself about yourself. I gave you an assignment (that you still need to do) to go into the bathroom, shut the door, look in the mirror, and have a hard conversation with yourself. But brutal honesty has to go further. It's time to be honest with someone else. Like the Prodigal Son, you may need to be honest with the person you've offended or sinned against. Chances are you've already thought of a dozen excuses for why this isn't necessary, but the more you protest internally, the more likely it is you need to sit down with them and talk.

I want to challenge you to pray to God to give you someone in your life with whom you can be brutally honest. The kind of person you are praying for is:

- a Christian who shares your convictions;
- someone who will be honest themselves;
- someone who is trustworthy;
- someone who has freely received the grace of Jesus and freely gives it.

Most Christians understand and accept the importance of being honest, both with themselves and with God. In 1 John, the Bible tells us that when we confess our sins to God, He is faithful and just to forgive us our sins and cleanse us from all unrighteousness. The Bible also says that Jesus took the punishment we deserve upon Himself when He died on the cross. Jesus died for my sins so that when I confess them, God forgives them.

Usually, we tell ourselves that it doesn't have to go any further than that: "If I'm honest with myself and with God, that's enough." But AHA requires more. In the New Testament book of James, we read:

> Therefore confess your sins to each other and pray
> for each other so that you may be healed. (5:16)

When we are honest with God about our sins, He forgives us, but when we are honest with others, we find healing.

What does *healing* mean?

Well, the practice of confessing our sins to one another holds us accountable and helps us find the encouragement we need to break the cycle of our struggle. When we take what we have kept in the dark and drag it kicking and screaming into the light, we find that it loses much of its power over us.

And the healing James talks about is more literal than you might think. Check this out: A secular, contemporary psychology textbook entitled *Coping with Stress* confirms the healing power of confession. The author claims that, "people who tend to keep secrets have more physical and mental complaints, on average, than people who do not … [including] greater anxiety, depression, and bodily symptoms such as back pain and headaches.… The initial embarrassment of confessing is frequently outweighed by the relief that comes with the verbalization of the darker secretive aspects of the self."[4]

---

4   C. R. Snyder, *Coping with Stress* (New York: Oxford University Press, 2001), 200, 205.

Proverbs 28:13 echoes these findings: "Whoever conceals their sins does not prosper, but the one who confesses and renounces them finds mercy."

Chapter 6

DENIAL—IF I IGNORE IT, MAYBE IT WILL GO AWAY

My wife and I recently watched one of those news-magazine shows that usually go like this:

1) Find the most disgusting thing people unknowingly encounter every day—say wood pulp in fast-food beef.
2) Make a half-hour exposé about it.

I know it sounds ridiculous, but it's the kind of show that if you watch for five minutes, you're hooked. In this particular episode, the reporter visited different hotels. Black light in hand, the reporter would walk into one of the rooms, and the purple glow of his truth-detecting light would illuminate all manner of germs and stains in the room, bright neon against the bedspread. This is the surest way I know for a husband to ruin all future romantic getaways with his wife.

In one of the more disturbing scenes, the reporter waited in the lobby looking for a victim. He finally cornered a poor, unsuspecting couple—probably enjoying what had thus far been a great vacation—and asked if they would submit their room to his black-light experiment. My wife and I were involuntarily talking to the TV at this point:

"Don't do it! This is going to ruin your anniversary! Run away now!"

Sadly, the couple agreed to take the crew up to their room. So the husband and wife, and the reporter and his camera crew, all crowded into the elevator. The reporter held back any indication that he knew what would happen. Meanwhile, this poor couple was on the verge of what would be a scarring moment, and they were obliviously making small talk about the museums in town. They got to the hotel room and walked in with the lights on. Everything looked pristine, as if room service had been there within the past hour. My wife and I commented on the cleanliness of the room, the crispness of the bedsheets.

This could be the one room that survived the test.

Suddenly, the lights went out and there was a moment of silence like you might expect in a movie theater just before the monster is revealed. The black light came on, and stains showed up everywhere. Unbelievably, it was even worse than the rooms shown previously. The neon glow was everywhere, including a suspiciously large stain on the carpet. As my wife and I groaned, we heard the couple start to panic. The wife began to scream. You'll never guess what she screamed over and over again: "Turn that off! Turn that off! Turn that off!"

After a few seconds, she rushed over to turn the lights back on herself. In an instant, everything looked normal again. She started to calm down, emitting some nervous laughter. "That's better," she said.

But, um … here's the thing—*the stains were still there.*

The couple could no longer see them, but that didn't change the reality of the stains' existence.

The word for this is *denial*. Denial is turning off the black light in an effort to make the stains disappear. You pretend that everything is okay even though everything is not okay. Sigmund Freud defined denial this way: denial is a defense mechanism in which a person is faced with a fact that is too uncomfortable to accept, so they reject it despite overwhelming evidence.

Instead of brutal honesty, many of us have chosen continued denial. We have been confronted with a reality that is so uncomfortable, so inconvenient, we choose to continue living in a false reality.

Recently I read about another example of denial. What do you think is the number-one way people respond when they get a bill in the mail that they don't have the money to pay? You guessed the answer: they don't open it.

The truth is too uncomfortable, so they pretend as though everything is okay. This is the same reason women who have a family history of breast cancer are sometimes the least likely to get a mammogram, or why men who have a family history of heart disease often ignore the warning signs. The evidence may be there, in fact, it may be overwhelming, but our response is:

"Turn that off!"

David's Denial

In 2 Samuel 11—12, David was king of Israel, his armies were at war, and they regularly conquered neighboring peoples and fortresses. In the realm of royalty, David was at the top of his game. During this season of success, David made some devastating mistakes, and then, instead of being honest about his secret sin, David chose denial.

It began one night when David was on the high roof of his palace. It was the custom of the day for women to bathe on their rooftops at certain hours of the night. As part of their ceremonial baths, they were only to bathe with water that had been naturally gathered. And of course, they weren't able to have hot water by turning the faucet knob to the letter H,[1] but water on the roof would have been kept warm by the sun.

Did David know what he would see when he stepped out onto that roof?

Perhaps this was David's version of getting up and flipping through pay-per-view channels. On this particular night, he saw a woman bathing, turned to his servant, and said, "Find out who this woman is for me."

The servant, however, already knew the answer. He replied, "She is Bathsheba." He didn't stop there. My guess is he swallowed hard before he added on the next part. "She is Bathsheba ... the *wife* of Uriah the Hittite" (2 Sam. 11:3, italics added). In other words,

---

1   Since we have four women in our home who like to take long, hot showers, I have taught my son that the letter H stands for "Hope you like it cold."

"David, the woman you're lusting over is the wife of one of your most trusted soldiers, who is fighting on the battlefield right now."

As I read about this rooftop moment, it seemed to me that God was waving a big red flag for David. He used a servant to try to get David's attention. David ignored the warning, invited Bathsheba to the palace, and had an affair with her.

A short time later, Bathsheba sent a three-word note that would change their lives forever: "I am pregnant" (v. 5). This should have been an awakening moment that would bring David to a place of brutal honesty. It was time to come clean and confess. But David was still in denial.

David schemed to bring Bathsheba's husband back from the battlefield. *Maybe,* he thought, *if Uriah sleeps with his wife, he'll assume the baby is his own.* After a few pleasantries about the troops, David sent Uriah home, expecting he'd do what any husband would after weeks away from his wife. But Uriah slept on his porch, a sign of solidarity for his fellow soldiers still at war.

When David found out about this act of integrity, it should have been a repentant moment. Seeing such integrity and honor in Uriah should have caused David to be honest with himself. It was time to stop living in denial. It was time to do the hard thing and confess his sin. Instead, he went deeper into denial.

David told Uriah to stay another day, and this time he got Uriah drunk. Pouring this faithful soldier the "wine that sent us reeling" (Ps. 60:3 NLT), David had another chance to be honest and open about his sin. But he continued with his plan, hoping that, in drunkenness, Uriah would yield to the lure of his wife's bedchambers. But Uriah didn't go home. And David realized that time was running out before Uriah returned to war. Suddenly David's options for dealing with the situation became fewer and more desperate.

Jim Collins writes about this ethical truth after studying business executives who've somehow gone wrong. He says, "If you would have told them ten years ahead of time, 'Hey, let's cook the books and get rich,' they would have never gone along with it." That's rarely how people get drawn into activities they later regret. He writes, "When you are at step A, it seems almost inconceivable to jump all the way to step Z. Step Z involves something that is a total breach of your values. But if you go from step A to step B to step C then to step D, someday you will wake up and discover you are at step Y and then the move to step Z becomes that much easier."[2]

So David found himself at step Y, but instead of choosing honesty, he chose a cover-up. He wrote a letter to his commander Joab, instructing him to put Uriah on the front lines of the fiercest fighting, then to pull back and let him be killed.

David handed the message to Uriah to deliver to his own commander—making the man unknowingly carry his own death sentence to the executioner.

Uriah was killed in battle, and David thought that maybe, just maybe, this was now over. Now he could move on and no one else had to know what he'd done.

Sometimes we wish that's how life worked, don't we?

If only ignoring the problem would make it go away. But many of us have learned that an unopened credit-card bill doesn't stave off

---

2   Jim Collins, "The Secret Life of the CEO," *Fast Company*, October 2002, http://www.jimcollins.com/article_topics/articles/the-secret-life.html.

problems. Instead, every day of denial only increases the balance, which will eventually have to be paid. Denial leads farther down a path than you ever imagined you would go.

Reality Check

We don't really know how long it took the Prodigal Son to wake up and recognize the reality of his situation. He landed this awful job, but he made no changes to his life. He got to the point of wanting to eat pig slop but still didn't make any changes. He stuck with that job for a while, despite the overwhelming evidence that things had gone terribly wrong.

What keeps a person in the pigpen? Denial.

Even though you're feeding pig slop to pigs;

even though your spouse has filed for divorce;

even though you haven't been sober for a week in years;

even though you make yourself the same promise every night;

even though you can't remember the last time you got on your knees and prayed …

you keep living like everything is going to be okay.

Notice in the parable what the younger son is honest about. He says in Luke 15:17, "Here I am starving to death!"

So take a minute and look around. Where are you? Define the reality of your circumstances. The word *reality* could be defined as "the state of things as they actually exist."

For example, someone might have an awakening that they need to do something differently financially. It's gotten bad. Changes should have been made a long time ago, but now the situation is desperate.

The person comes to his senses. Well, coming to one's senses is one thing, but it's another thing to be honest about reality. However, being honest is the essential next step. This person must tell himself the truth about his current financial reality. That means looking at where he's spending money, acknowledging unnecessary and frivolous purchases, and going through all his debts and laying them out on the table.

It's humiliating.

It's embarrassing.

It's painful.

It's essential.

But this is where so many of us get stuck. We have an awakening, but we lack the courage to be brutally honest with ourselves about our current reality.

Three Tactics of Denial

1. Disagree

Have you ever been in a discussion with someone who was blatantly wrong, but they still disagreed with you? Eventually it became clear that their disagreement has less to do with the facts and more to do with what they want to be true. It's the old adage, "Don't bother me with the facts; my mind's already made up."

A number of years ago, I was talking to a young man who had grown up in my church and was home on college break. When I ran into him, I asked him how his freshman year was going, and he asked if we could sit down and talk for a few minutes.

Here's how he began the conversation: "Hey, I wanted to talk to you, because over the last few months, I've been studying Scripture, and I have come to the conclusion that sex before marriage is not a sin."

He was intelligent and articulate, and he attempted to give me his reasoning. Then I pointed him to a few passages of Scripture from Thessalonians and Hebrews about honoring marriage and the intimacy of marriage, and we talked about some Greek words and some different meanings of sex and the oneness God had in mind for marriage.

After we talked for a while, he finally said, "Look, maybe that is what it meant for the people in that time, but a lot of things have changed, so the meaning of this has changed. I don't think what was true for them is true for us anymore. It's just a cultural difference."

Even though this kid knew what was biblical and right, he wanted to couch his decision to sin in the context of a disagreement about how to interpret the text. I finally said, "Look, I don't know you all that well, and I don't know much about your life, but let me make a guess here. You grew up being taught that sex outside of marriage is against God's will. Is that true?"

He said, "Yeah, that's true. I grew up thinking it is a sin. But I don't believe that anymore. I don't think it's a sin."

I said, "Okay, let me make one other guess—if that's okay. My guess is that you've gotten yourself a girlfriend … and you're sleeping with her. Is that true?"

Silence.

Finally he said, "Yeah, but that doesn't have anything to do with this."

That's denial.

We tell ourselves a lie, because the lie is more convenient to believe.

As Blaise Pascal is purported to have said, "People almost invariably arrive at their beliefs not on the basis of proof but on the basis of what they find attractive." In other words, we're willing to lie to ourselves about our reality and about what we believe if it means we can have something we want.

The Bible calls the moment when we have a moment of brutal honesty and we tell ourselves the truth—even when it's not what we want to hear—confession. AHA doesn't happen without it. There are a number of ways the word *confession* can be understood and defined, but here's one definition of confession: to agree. You come to a place where you stop disagreeing with truth and you honestly say, "Here I am."

2. Defend

I have a friend who is a personal trainer. I try not to have friends like this, but somehow it happened. The truth is that even though we are friends, I find myself avoiding him during seasons when I've gotten out of shape.[3] I feel bad around him, because I look at him and his cut arms and brick-wall build, and then I look down at my pudgy midsection and just hate life for a few seconds. But then I get a cookie-dough Blizzard and everything is okay.

Inevitably, when I am with him, I get the feeling that he is staring at my gut. He will usually ask me, "How's your diet and exercise routine going?" He asks it without judgment and I am sure out of

---

3   i.e., the past nine years.

genuine concern, but I still get defensive. I'll say, "I don't know, how's your prayer life and Scripture memorization going? How's that routine going *for you?*"

Of course I say this from a safe distance.

Defensiveness often reveals an area of our lives where we're in denial. So most of us avoid the personal trainers. We want to avoid the people and places that force us to be brutally honest. I've discovered that this is often why people have significant lapses in church attendance. I'll talk to people who come back to church after being away from it for a period of months or years, and they'll usually say something like:

"When I went to college, I started partying, and I guess that was about the time I stopped going to church …"

"I started dating this guy, and it wasn't long after that when I stopped going to church …"

"My marriage was falling apart, and it was about the same time I filed for divorce that I stopped going to church …"

I'm not even sure they realize the connection they are making. They avoided the people and places that might confront them with the truth about where they were.

That tends to be how we respond to stains in our lives. We are convicted of them. The light of God's Word illuminates them, shines on them. We recognize: *Oh, look at these stains.* But we don't want to deal with them, so we just keep God's light away from the corners of our lives and pretend as though everything is okay. We try to maintain this illusion. We avoid honest moments because sometimes the truth hurts. Here's the rub: AHA won't happen until we come to a place where we stop defending ourselves.

3. Distract

It's easy for us to live in denial about one part of our life if the other parts are keeping us busy and going well. That must have been true for King David. David's personal life may have been falling apart, but professionally things were going well. The nation of Israel was experiencing some of its best days. They'd defeated their enemies and the kingdom was flourishing.

It's the workaholic who gets a job promotion and is awarded Salesman of the Year, but he's completely oblivious to the fact that his teenage son is smoking pot and his wife feels completely alone.

It's the mother who keeps a beautiful home. She is constantly decorating and cleaning, but doesn't seem to notice that her children just go to their rooms and shut their doors.

It's the twentysomething who knows every TV-show reference but fails to take notice that all his friendships are becoming more and more shallow, no longer based on things that actually matter.

That last example hits home for me a little, because as I mentioned in the opening of this chapter, I've been sucked into TV shows before. There's a show I sometimes watch called *Kitchen Nightmares*.

If you haven't seen the show, here's the premise: a world-class chef steps into restaurants that are—you guessed it—living nightmares. The restaurants are typically on the verge of closing and in desperate need of help. What's interesting is that sometimes the restaurants look appealing from the outside. Often, large amounts of time and money have been spent finding the right location and creating a welcoming atmosphere. But in every episode, the real problem is the same: the food is nasty.

One of the painfully entertaining parts of every show is how the show's host, Gordon Ramsay, tries over and over to get the restaurant workers to realize they are in an Oh no! situation. The owners have typically already had a sudden awakening, because the business is in trouble, but what they need is some brutal honesty. And Chef Ramsay is brutal. He'll usually order about a half-dozen items off the menu and with great passion and clarity explain how horrible each one tastes.

The restaurant owners are in denial about the quality of their food because they are distracted by everything else going on. They're managing food orders, overseeing waitstaff, stepping out of the kitchen to shake hands with customers—basically anything but actually making good food. The show is half over before any of them get honest about reality.

We said earlier the word *reality* could be defined as "the state of things as they actually exist." That can be difficult and painful, but more often than not, experiencing AHA begins with an Oh no! moment.

David's Oh No! Moment

A year passed, and King David continued to live in denial. He reigned successfully, penning psalms and winning wars, but he had yet to truly acknowledge his sin. He'd tucked it away, fenced it off. He hadn't been honest and hadn't been broken over it. God had given him time, but he still hadn't confessed, so God sent the prophet Nathan to have a "Chef Ramsay moment" with David.

Nathan went to King David and said, "David, a situation has come up. There are two men in your kingdom. One man is wealthy and has all kinds of sheep, a great herd. But his neighbor is poor and has only one lamb. This lamb is like a child to the poor man, because he has nothing else. The lamb eats the food off his table and sleeps at the foot of his bed. But David, here's what happened: The rich man, the one with all the sheep, he had a friend over, and they decided that for dinner, they really wanted a rack of lamb. Instead of killing one of his own sheep, the rich man went over to his poor neighbor's house and took that lamb. He stole it, barbecued it, and served it to his friend. What should we do here, David?"

David was furious. He demanded justice for the poor man and said, "The man who did this deserves to die!" Then Nathan stopped him and said four words:

"You are that man."

After multiple cover-ups and a year of denial, David finally broke. He was finally honest with himself, Nathan, and God.

Confession is the only cure for denial.

Every one of us would prefer to skip this part of AHA. After we have the sudden awakening, we are ready to move on with our lives. But lasting change and true transformation require confession. The word for *confession* in the New Testament most commonly means, "to acknowledge." You acknowledge the reality of your situation.

Psalm 51 is a record of David's prayer of confession. Through brokenness and tears, David finally told the truth to himself and to God. You'll notice he references the "stains" in his life. But his response to the stains was no longer to turn off the lights and pretend as though everything was okay. No, he turned on the black light, exposed the stain, and asked God to wash him clean.

Have mercy on me, O God,

    because of your unfailing love.

Because of your great compassion,

    blot out the stain of my sins.

Wash me clean from my guilt.

    Purify me from my sin.

For I recognize my rebellion;

    it haunts me day and night.

Against you, and you alone, have I sinned;

    I have done what is evil in your sight.

You will be proved right in what you say,

    and your judgment against me is just.

For I was born a sinner—

    yes, from the moment my mother conceived me.

But you desire honesty from the womb,

    teaching me wisdom even there.

Purify me from my sins, and I will be clean;

    wash me, and I will be whiter than snow.

Oh, give me back my joy again;

    you have broken me—

    now let me rejoice.

Don't keep looking at my sins.

    Remove the stain of my guilt. (NLT)

Stop.

Before you go to the next chapter, read Psalm 51 again. But this time, instead of reading David's words, *pray them*.

Chapter 7

PROJECTION—IT'S NOT MY FAULT, SO IT'S NOT MY RESPONSIBILITY

Have you noticed that there are more and more warning signs everywhere you look? Do you know why all these warning labels exist? Most likely because at some point, someone sued the company over that particular issue.

How do you explain the labels that come on our coffee cups that read, "Caution: Coffee May Be Hot." Somebody probably burned her mouth or spilled hot coffee on herself and then sued the restaurant. Ever see the stroller warning label that says, "Warning: Remove infant before folding stroller for storage"? Wow. Some parent[1] absentmindedly folded up his toddler and sued the company for it. A Batman costume has a warning that reads, "Warning: Cape does

---

1 ~~Parent~~ Dad

not enable user to fly." First of all, everyone knows Batman doesn't fly. That's Superman. But some kid must've gotten on the top bunk and launched spread-eagle across his bedroom, probably breaking a femur in the process. Mom came running in and said, "Does that costume not have a warning label on it?!"

If you don't believe me, look them up.

After finding these online, I couldn't help but notice warnings on items around my house. The worst one I found was in my garage. The warning label on my chainsaw says, "Do not attempt to stop chain with hands."

Our society has become masterful about blaming others for our own foolish choices. Instead of being brutally honest with ourselves, most of us want to place the blame on others. The word for this is *projection*. Projection is when we admit the reality of an unpleasant fact, but we deny responsibility. Denial is refusing to admit the reality of an unpleasant fact, but projection is admitting that the reality exists without taking responsibility for it. We just blame someone else.

This approach is as old as time.

Go back to the book of Genesis, where we read about the first man and woman, Adam and Eve. They lived a beautiful life in a garden called Eden. The garden was full of beautiful trees that produced delicious fruit. In Genesis 2:16–17, God specifically and clearly told them what they were not permitted to do:

> But the LORD God warned him, "You may freely eat the fruit of every tree in the garden—except the tree of the knowledge of good and evil. If you eat its fruit, you are sure to die." (NLT)

You remember what happened. The Devil came on the scene and did what he does best. He lied. He told them they were missing out by not eating the fruit of that tree and the only reason God had told them they couldn't is because He didn't want them to be like Him.

The Bible says that Eve took a big bite of the fruit. She told Adam it was delicious, and he took a bite. God confronted Adam and asked, "Have you eaten from the tree that I commanded you not to eat from?" (Gen. 3:11). *Boom.* That's a sudden awakening. So how did Adam respond? Here's what Adam said:

> Yes, God. I confess. I broke Your command. I have
> sinned and not obeyed Your word. Here and now I
> take responsibility for my rebellion. I don't deserve
> it, but I humbly ask You for Your grace and mercy.

Okay, so that's not exactly how it went. When God confronted Adam in verse 12, here's what happened:

> The man said, "The woman you put here with me—
> she gave me some fruit from the tree, and I ate it."

That's projection.

Instead of being honest and confessing his sin, Adam said to God, "That woman you put here with me …" In other words, "God, this isn't my fault. It's her fault."

My wife is a bit of a handywoman, and when she's in a fix-it mood but needs ideas for a project, she'll watch the DIY Network. I don't choose to watch this with her very often, but one show I get a kick out of is called *Renovation Realities*. Each episode focuses on a couple who takes on a remodeling project. Like most reality shows, it is predictable. The enjoyment comes in watching the inevitable train wreck reach its conclusion. The couples participating clearly don't watch the show, because if they'd seen even one episode, they would know that no couple has ever escaped a renovation unscathed.

Here is how it starts.

The couple gives each other a kiss and a high five, and they begin the remodel. Initially, they pull down the cabinets, making quick work of the ugly plywood they are replacing. Cue nondescript celebratory music as they celebrate their progress. However, by the commercial break, it all goes wrong. The new wood they've purchased is not the right stain, but they damaged it during the install attempt. Then the producers show a clip of the wife, who is not happy. She'll say something like, "I knew this was a bad idea." But she didn't. The husband will say something like, "I've got this under control." But he doesn't. And everything is a mess. The new cabinetry looks awful, having been installed at an accidental incline. Seeing this, the wife blames the husband for his poor measurements, while the husband blames the wife for ordering the wrong size.

That was Adam's approach too. There was only one other person on the planet with him, and he blamed her. He also blamed God, because He was the one who created Eve. After confronting Adam, God confronted Eve, who in verse 13 of chapter 3, responded the same way Adam had.

> Then the LORD God said to the woman, "What is
> this you have done?"

The woman said, "The serpent deceived me, and I ate."

When confronted with the truth, instead of being brutally honest, they each pointed the finger of blame at someone or something else.

Honest about Responsibility

Projection is when we follow our sudden awakening with excuses and justifications. So instead of accepting responsibility, we assign blame:

I know it was wrong to change the numbers, but my boss has unrealistic expectations.

I know it was wrong to plagiarize in my paper, but everyone does it.

I was wrong to lose my temper, but you should have seen the home I grew up in.

I was wrong to be disrespectful to my husband, but he is so passive.

I know it's wrong for me to look at that stuff, but my wife doesn't even try anymore.

Try this. Just say these four words:
"I am a sinner."

Say it again. This time out loud:
"I am a sinner."

Instead of staying in denial or projecting his mistakes on someone else, the Prodigal Son was honest about his reality and said,

"Here I am starving to death." He said, "I have sinned." There is something beautiful about that short phrase. Those three words set him on a path to freedom.

The Blame Game

As I studied the Prodigal Son, I was struck by all the different people in the story he could have blamed for the position he found himself in but didn't. He could've taken on the role of the victim in all of this and said, "It's not my fault," and then pointed the finger at someone else.

He could have blamed his friends. We read that the Prodigal Son went to a distant country where he spent all of his money on partying. It's safe to assume that he blew through his money buying drinks for a group of newly acquired friends. When the money disappeared, they did too.

He could have blamed the pig farmer. He could have complained that he wasn't being treated fairly. Never mind a fair day's wage, the farmer wouldn't even let him satisfy his appetite with the food the pigs were eating.

Instead of looking at these two examples, I want us to closely consider who I think would have been the two most likely prospects for his projection:

The father

Don't you think the Prodigal Son could've blamed his dad for being too permissive or too passive? After all, what kind of father just gives his child his inheritance when it's asked for?

Mom and Dad tend to be easy targets when it comes to projection. Instead of taking responsibility, many people become bitter and blame their parents for the way they were raised. And sometimes it only seems fair.

I remember my parents giving us chocolate bunnies for Easter when I was a kid. I specifically remember hoping every year, *Maybe this Easter my parents will spend the extra money and get the* solid *chocolate bunny.* But every year ended in disappointment. Every year it was hollow. My dad would try to spiritualize the moment: "Yes, son, it's hollow on the inside. It's empty, just like the tomb on that first Easter morning." So as a child I learned to equate the resurrection of Christ with bitterness and disappointment. Thanks, Dad.

Okay, I'll admit that's probably a little harsh.

However, I have begun to listen for this kind of projection when I talk to people who need to make a change in their lives. I listened to a single mom in her mid-thirties who had no trouble being honest about her reality. She had been in and out of relationships her whole life. The longest she ever held the same job was eighteen months. She admitted to treating her depression by shopping. Consequently, she'd racked up all kinds of credit-card debt. But in the first two minutes of the conversation, she told me, "What am I supposed to do? I can't change my childhood, can I?"

She went on to tell me about parents who had divorced when she was young and how she hadn't really seen her father much after that. Her mom had had guys in and out of the house. Her dad remarried and started a new life. On the rare occasions she would visit his new family, she never felt like she was part of it. Several times she would be asked to take a picture of her dad and his new family, but she was almost never included. After defining reality for five minutes, she spent about fifteen blaming her parents.

It wasn't hard for me to sympathize with her. The truth is, her parents did a lot of things wrong and deeply wounded her when she was young and vulnerable. But did her parents rack up the credit-card debt? Did her parents make her quit a dozen jobs? Did her parents tell her who she was to date? Instead of being honest with herself, she was stuck in the pigpen of projection. As long as she continued to say, "It's not my fault," and blamed her parents, true AHA wouldn't happen.

Projection is especially common in marriages.

A marriage starts having trouble, and one spouse blames the other. Nothing has really changed since that first marriage in Genesis. Instead of taking responsibility, we point out what our spouse is doing wrong. I've listened as husbands and wives confess affairs or admit to abuse, both with no remorse because they have convinced themselves that they are the victim. They make it sound as if they had no choice based on the way their spouse treated them.

We all have a tendency toward projection in marriage. Instead of taking responsibility, we blame our spouse. Imagine that every day you take a lunch with you to work, and every day it's the same thing—chicken salad sandwiches. You continually complain to your coworkers that it's always chicken salad sandwiches in your lunch. You are sick and tired of chicken salad sandwiches. You even tell a coworker you'd rather die than eat one more chicken salad sandwich. Finally someone asks, "Why don't you ask your wife to make you something else?"

You reply, "Oh, actually I make lunch myself."

That's the reality for many of us. We end up in the Distant Country living in very difficult circumstances, and we make it sound like it's someone else's fault, when in reality, we've made our own lunch.

I read about an exercise a few years ago, which I did with my wife, and which helped us be honest with ourselves about ourselves instead of pointing the finger at each other. I got out a piece of paper and asked my wife to draw a circle on it.[2] In the circle we wrote down all the problems and challenges we were having in our marriage. Then each of us was to take a pen and carve out the piece of the pie that represented our responsibilities for the problems and challenges. Since this would have been uncomfortable, we both agreed that this part of the exercise was rhetorical in nature. It was just meant to make a point, and we didn't actually have to draw a piece of the pie. It was too hard to be honest with ourselves about the problems we were responsible for. But we could each probably have drawn the piece of the pie on behalf of the other person. Why? Projection is

---

2 I asked her because, without a protractor, I'm incapable of drawing a circle. I'll prove it:

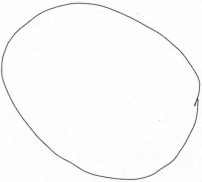

much easier than brutal honesty. The problem is that it doesn't get you out of the pigpen.

God

Between the famine in the land and not being able to find a decent job, it would have been easy for the Prodigal Son to blame God for his current condition. God rarely gets credit when things are going well, but He often gets blamed when times are tough.

A few years ago, I pulled into a crowded store parking lot. After maneuvering through the rows of cars, I finally found a spot. It may or may not have been a compact-car spot, but I was going to park my truck there no matter what. I squeezed into the spot, sighing with relief. Looking at the sky and seeing ominous storm clouds swirling overhead, I needed to hurry. The wind was picking up, and I was not going to be stuck on the road when the clouds unleashed rain.

Ready to make my quick trip, I started to get out of the truck. As I opened the door, the wind literally took it out of my hands. I watched my truck door slam into the car next to me, a relatively new-looking Toyota Camry.

I left my insurance information for the owner of the car, thinking I would have to pay for the damages. A few days later, I was on the phone with my insurance agent, explaining to him what happened and how the wind had ripped the door out of my hands. And he said something that shocked me. He said, "Well, this isn't your fault." I told him there was no way it was the other guy's fault because he was in the store at the time.

My agent replied, "No, it's not your fault, because this is what we call an act of God."

I said, "Really, this is God's fault? We can blame Him for this?" And it turns out that *act of God* is a legal term. So instead of taking responsibility for parking too close and not hanging on to the door tight enough, I got to blame God.

And that's what many of us do. If your marriage doesn't meet your expectations; if your child rebels; if you lose your job; if the economy collapses; if there is a famine in the land—we call it an act of God.

In fact, just this week as I've been working on this book, a terrifyingly powerful tornado hit just south of Oklahoma City in Moore, Oklahoma. The news coverage has been comprehensive, and the loss of homes and lives tragic. One particular video has gone viral. In it, a family is in a crawl space, and they have yet to come out after the storm. The husband holds the camera, and the darkness is washed out as he opens the storm hatch. He swings the camera left and right, and what used to be a neighborhood is now a flattened scrap heap. For thirty seconds or so, he just walks around, surveying the devastation, stunned into silence by the scene. When he finally speaks, he says, "The Lord giveth and the Lord taketh away." He was quoting the biblical character Job (see Job 1:21), a man who experienced the same level of devastation.

I couldn't help but notice the comment section underneath the video. There was a furious argument about whether or not this was God's fault. Some posted statements defending God, citing verses about God's love and mercy. Others declared with great assurance that this was not of God but of the Devil. Others blamed it on Mother Nature, saying we live in a harsh world. But the general consensus was that this *was* God's fault. When people don't know how to make sense of something or whom to blame, God becomes an easy target.

The Prodigal Son could have blamed God. Instead he was brutally honest and told himself the truth. He said, "I have sinned." If he had not rebelled against his father, he would have been well taken care of at home. If he had not spent all his money on wild living, he would have been able to get through a difficult famine.

He could've blamed God for the factors that were out of his control, but instead he took responsibility for what he could control, went home, and apologized to his father.

This kind of apology is rare, but it is pure and honest. Generally speaking, the shorter an apology, the better. We often lengthen our apologies to remove the full weight of responsibility. We're only willing to accept our portion of the blame if we know others are being handed their slice of the pie.

It's my fault, but if you hadn't …
I am sorry, and you should be too …
I messed up, but it was based on what you said …

But there's something powerful and cleansing in that simple act of dropping any embellishments to your admission of guilt. "No ifs, ands, or buts," as Mom would say.

Is there something you need to take responsibility for? Maybe there's someone who needs to hear you accept fault—not as a run-on sentence full of excuses but the short, simple, and powerful truth.

Chapter 8

MINIMIZE—IT'S NOT THAT BIG OF A DEAL

I was sitting in a coffee shop with my MacBook open on the table in front of me working on my sermon for the upcoming weekend. I was just wrapping it up when an older gentleman from the church came over, set his coffee cup on the table, extended his hand, and introduced himself to me. As he began talking with me, he accidently knocked over his coffee, which spilled right onto my keyboard. I watched in horror as twenty ounces of fresh coffee soaked my computer. The screen almost immediately flashed and shut off.

When I looked at the man, it was clear he didn't realize what he had done. He chuckled and said, "Oh, sorry about that," and tottered off to grab a fistful of napkins before returning to dab the keyboard, sopping up the coffee.

Meanwhile, I was in shock. Everything was in slow motion. It became an out-of-body experience. I kept thinking, *Is this really happening?* Still on napkin duty, the older man tried to lighten the mood. He pointed to the Apple logo on my Mac and said, "Looks like someone already took a bite out of that apple anyway."

He had a good laugh at that one.

I grabbed my computer, shut it, and practically ran away. I didn't even know where I was going. I could feel the hot coffee coming out of my MacBook. I was thinking of everything on my hard drive that still needed to be backed up. Including my sermon for that weekend.

A few days later, he called my office to apologize, and then he said, "I hope your computer dried out, and it didn't end up being a big deal." I didn't have the heart to tell him the truth. He still jokes with me about it every now and then, because to him, it was just a small accident.

That's minimization—though in this case unintentional.

Denial is refusing to acknowledge the reality of a situation. Projection is acknowledging the reality of the situation but denying any responsibility. Minimization is acknowledging the reality of the situation and even owning responsibility for it but denying its seriousness.

Instead of being brutally honest, we tell ourselves partial and palatable truths. We tell ourselves, "It's not that bad." In the words of the Black Knight after Arthur cut off both of his arms: "It's only a flesh wound."[1]

It wasn't until things were really bad that the Prodigal Son finally told himself the truth. He said, "Here I am starving to death!" He acknowledged just how desperate his situation was. He had plenty of

---

1   Terry Gilliam and Terry Jones, *Monty Python and the Holy Grail* (Python [Monty] Pictures, 1975).

opportunities to be honest with himself along the way, but he never seemed to realize the seriousness of the situation. Yet in this moment of brutal honesty he practiced the speech he would give his father upon returning home. And in the speech in Luke 15:18–19, he told the truth about where his sin and rebellion had led:

> Father, I have sinned against heaven and against you. I am no longer worthy to be called your son; make me like one of your hired servants.

I'm not sure who first said it, but there is an old saying about what sin always does. It goes likes this:

> *Sin will always take you farther than you want to go.*
> *Sin will always cost you more than you want to pay.*
> *Sin will always keep you longer than you want to stay.*

Scripture doesn't minimize the consequences of sin. We repeatedly see just how seriously God takes it. In the Old Testament, when God wanted to warn the people that destruction was coming, He would most often send a prophet. The prophet would confront the people with the truth of where things were heading. The people would frequently minimize the prophet's message. Instead of repenting and turning back to God, they would continue down the same path. But when the people were brutally honest and repented of their sin, God would respond with compassion and grace.

For example, God sent Jonah to Nineveh to warn the people of coming destruction. Jonah traveled into the city, and in Jonah 3:4, he gave them God's message. Here's the sermon he preached to the people:

Forty more days and Nineveh will be overthrown.

It might be the shortest sermon in the history of the world. It's only eight words long. Actually I checked this sermon in the original Hebrew, and in that language, it's only six words long. Jonah showed up and started preaching that in forty days the city would be destroyed.

Jonah didn't minimize the message. He didn't open up with a joke to ease the tension. He didn't make any effort to find something positive to balance out his message. He didn't apologize for hurting their feelings.

Sometimes, as a pastor, in an effort to avoid upsetting people, I tend to lighten the full brunt of the truth. There's a temptation to avoid using words like *sin, sinner, hell,* and *punishment.* But as I write this, I am convicted once again that perhaps one of the reasons people minimize sin is because preachers don't seem to take it seriously. Jonah's message was direct and straightforward: "You've got a little more than a month, then it's lights-out for you, Nineveh." Apparently it was enough. The next three words in verse 5 changed everything for Nineveh. We read simply:

The Ninevites believed ...

They didn't minimize the situation. They didn't say to themselves, "Oh, Jonah's exaggerating to get our attention. I'm sure it won't be that bad." They didn't say, "Forty days? That's plenty of time. I'm sure things will get better." Instead we read that the people believed. It was hard to hear, but they embraced Jonah's brutal honesty.

Instead of being honest, we tend to minimize. We minimize not only our responsibility but also the repercussions of the decisions we've made. *Minimization* is not a word we use often, but there are some phrases I'm sure the Prodigal Son would have told himself and that we often tell ourselves when we minimize the reality of a situation.

I'm Just Having Fun

This is a favorite saying of those in the Distant Country. The Prodigal Son spent all his money on wild living, but hey, he was just having a good time. We rationalize by telling ourselves, "As long as I'm having fun and not hurting anyone, it's fine."

There is a book entitled *Over the Edge: Death in Grand Canyon*. As you might guess, it's not a real uplifting read. The author chronicles the nearly seven hundred deaths that have taken place at the Grand Canyon since the 1870s. What was surprising to me was not *that* so many people have died there but *how* many of the deaths occurred. A number of people have fallen to their deaths simply because they were joking around.

In 1992 a thirty-eight-year-old father was teasing his teenage daughter and pretended to lose his balance and fall, laughing at the gag. One second he was pranking his daughter, then suddenly the fake fall became very real. He stumbled a bit too far and fell four hundred feet to his death.

More recently, in 2012, an eighteen-year-old young lady was hiking around the North Rim with friends and thought it would be fun to have her picture taken next to the edge where there was a sign that read, "Stay Away." Just an ironic picture for Facebook to show she was a true adventurer. As she clambered to where the sign stood, several rocks gave way beneath her, and she fell 1,500 feet.

As a pastor I've discovered that people often blow off warnings by minimizing consequences. In their minds, they are just having fun. But what we don't realize is that it's all leading somewhere. The Prodigal Son was living it up in the Distant Country, but he was closer to the edge than he realized and eventually the rocks gave way. They always do.

In tears, a woman told me how, because of an affair, she lost everything: her marriage, family, and relationship with her kids. With tears running down her cheeks, she shook her head and said to me, "It just started with some harmless flirting at work."

The journey to the pigpen almost always starts when we minimize our sin.

"I'm just having fun."

Things Will Get Better

I'm sure the Prodigal Son must have told himself this multiple times. When he ran low on money, when his food supply dwindled, when he couldn't find a decent job, or perhaps on his first day in the pigpen, he told himself, "It's not that bad. I'm sure things will get better."

Another way I sometimes hear this is, "I'm sure things can't get any worse than this." I wonder if that is what Pharaoh told himself after each of the first nine plagues. As things spiral farther down, instead of being brutally honest, we often continue to minimize the situation. We keep saying, "Things will get better," but the truth is that things have never been worse.

And I can't help but wonder, *What's it gonna take?*

What's it gonna take for you to realize how bad things have gotten?

What's it gonna take for you to admit that your marriage is falling apart?

What's it gonna take for you to get some help for your addiction?

What's it gonna take for you to realize you're losing your kids?

What's it gonna take for you to seek God's help?

Seriously, how far does this have to go?

It's Not that Big of a Deal

This would have been the likely response from the Prodigal Son if someone had tried to warn him about where his decisions were leading. In fact, *It's not that big of a deal* is a phrase I have often heard when confronting someone about the choices they are making.

Have you ever seen the TV show *Hoarders*? The show usually features people in danger of losing their homes, or even their kids, all because so much junk has piled up in their house that it is no longer safe to live in. The footage can be shocking. The camera crew opens the door to a home, and they can barely get inside the house. A small path winds through rooms that are packed wall-to-wall with newspapers, dirty clothes, composting food, unopened boxes, unidentifiable collectibles, unrecognizable rot, and trash.

I should mention I'm not the neatest or most organized person, so whenever I watch the show, I try to make sure my wife is paying attention, because I gotta believe the messiness of the hoarders makes me look really good. But here's what I've noticed about *Hoarders*: there inevitably comes a point in the program when the hoarder is being interviewed about the state of their home. They typically offer one of two responses. Sometimes they say, "I'm not sure how it got to be like this." But the other common response is: "I really don't think it's that bad."

They can't access the bedroom. They can't use the bathroom. No one can see the bed, the table, the countertops, or the floor, because there are piles and piles of stuff everywhere. But their response is still: "It's not that big of a deal."

The problem is we don't realize how bad things are. When you spend too much time in the Distant Country, you start to compare yourself to the people around you, saying, "If everyone is living this way, then what's the big deal?" It's the slippery slope of the Distant Country. Soon your perspective becomes warped. After spending enough time in Nineveh, the sin and rebellion doesn't seem like a big deal because everyone is doing it. And when everyone is doing it, it's harder to be brutally honest about your own condition.

About ten years ago, we moved into a neighborhood where no one took great care of their lawns. We all mowed when we got around to it. No one fertilized or specially treated their grass. There were a lot of weeds. We seemed to have an unspoken agreement that dandelions were actually beautiful flowers, and the more you had, the prettier your yard looked. And we were all quite content and happy living this way. Then one day a new neighbor moved in next door. We'll call him

Jonah. Anyway, Jonah began to take meticulous care of his grass. Have you ever had a neighbor like that? They use dark magic to give their lawn some checked pattern? That's not of God. If He wanted grass to be checkered, He would have made it that way.

You may think that having a neighbor with a beautiful lawn is great, but you know what? It was annoying. Jonah's yard revealed the truth about our yards. His commitment to excellence was an indictment against our commitment to mediocrity. And it just took the one neighbor coming in and holding up a different standard for the rest of us to be more honest about what a mess things had become.

In large part, this was the purpose for Old Testament law. God revealed His perfect standard to us, and we realized just how bad things were. God's Word is meant to get our attention so we won't minimize our sin, but rather realize the seriousness of the situation.

God's Word should get our attention and help us see that some things are a bigger deal than we previously realized. As I was growing up my mother taught me to listen attentively when God's Word was being read and taught.

It wasn't always that way. Like many church kids I spent my earliest years sitting with my parents in "big church." When the sermon started, my mom would give me a snack to keep me quiet. Want to guess what the snack was? Yep. Cheerios. It's the official snack of moms who want their kids to be quiet. So I would take my little baggie of Cheerios, and I would stretch out on the pew while the pastor taught God's Word. Cheerios are great from that standpoint, because there's this little hole in them. One can't choke on a Cheerio when they're lying down in the pew. But I remember lying there, counting all the lights in the ceiling, waiting for the sermon to be over.

However, at some point, my mother tried to teach me to listen attentively and take seriously the Word of God. So when I was too old to lie down in the pew with Cheerios, she required me to sit next to her and pay attention, which was difficult for me. But my mom had this crazy ability. She could listen to the sermon with a pleasant and attentive look on her face, taking notes and nodding her head, and at the same time she could pinch the underside of my thigh to remind me to be still and listen. She was an expert at this. She could pinch me with just the right amount of pressure so that when I screamed, nothing came out, but not so hard it would draw blood and create a mess.

There is a tendency for us to minimize the Word of the Lord. Maybe because of its familiarity. "Familiarity breeds contempt," the saying goes. But it may be more accurate to say that "familiarity breeds indifference." The more we hear some warnings, the less seriously we take them—like the tornado warnings in grade school we didn't take seriously. The people of Nineveh heard God's warning. God got their attention, and they were honest with themselves *about* themselves. One of the reasons we minimize our own sin and rebellion is that we don't take God's Word seriously. Maybe a strong pinch is needed to get us to sit up and pay attention.

Confronted with the Truth

When Jonah confronted the people of Nineveh with the truth, how did they respond? With brutal honesty.

Jonah 3:5 records:

> A fast was proclaimed, and all of them, from the
> greatest to the least, put on sackcloth.

Sackcloth was an abrasive covering made of goat hair that was worn in public as a sign of repentance and grieving. Does that sound like something a respectable person would wear? Is that something you would do? Well here, even the people of privilege and power did this.

Picture Donald Trump publicly fasting. Think of Kim Kardashian putting on sackcloth. This was a gesture of humility. Remember, this was a great city in Assyria with around 120 thousand people, and everyone—from the greatest to the least—fasted and put on sackcloth. When news reached the king of Nineveh, he rose from his throne, and he, too, put on sackcloth and fasted. But he didn't stop there. He issued the following decree:

> By the decree of the king and his nobles:
> Do not let people or animals, herds or flocks, taste
> anything; do not let them eat or drink. But let people
> and animals be covered with sackcloth. Let everyone
> call urgently on God. Let them give up their evil ways
> and their violence. Who knows? God may yet relent
> and with compassion turn from his fierce anger so
> that we will not perish. (Jon. 3:7–9)

The point is that the people did not take this lightly. Try putting sackcloth on your cat sometime. That's hardcore repentance.

The people of Nineveh didn't minimize the seriousness of Jonah's message; instead they were brutally honest with themselves.

Jonah 3:10 tells us that when God saw what they did and how they turned from their wicked ways, He did not bring upon them the destruction He had threatened.

Instead of minimizing, the people of Nineveh were honest with themselves about themselves. They recognized that their sin was a big deal, and they responded to that truth with confession, repentance, and brokenness.

Instead of telling himself, "It's no big deal" or "I'm sure things will get better," the Prodigal Son told himself the truth about himself. He didn't minimize his rebellion or the consequences he deserved. He was honest in counting the cost of his choices. He said very plainly, "I'm no longer worthy to be called your son." He recognized the relational damage he had done. The son had wounded his father's pride and scarred their relationship in a way that was nearly irreparable. And he recognized the full weight of that emotional damage. In walking away from his father, the son had also walked away from the family as a whole. He had walked away from his brother, his parents, and his community.

I remember when a friend of mine, a pastor at a large church, made some very unfortunate and public mistakes. His choices cost him his job and his family, and he ended up going through an expensive divorce. As the dust settled from his disastrous fall, he took the time to count the cost—*literally*. He added up every economic asset and material possession he had lost, including the salary from the years he would have stayed in that position. It was well over half a million dollars. Not counting the moral and relational consequences, my buddy realized that even in the most practical sense, his sin had cost him everything. That's brutal honesty, and AHA doesn't happen without it.

So what about you? Add up your bill. What is the true cost of your sin?

Paul tells us that, "The wages of sin is death." That's the bill. Our choice to sin has created a barrier between us and God, taken a toll on our relationship with Him that we can't fix, repair, or pay off on our own. Let's not minimize the situation. We've lived in offense to a holy, righteous God, who reigns in justice. We deserve death for what we've done. Like the Prodigal Son, we've robbed honor from our Father. We have scorned His provision and fled from His house. We have chosen wild living with strangers over a relationship with Him. Like the Prodigal Son, we've told God we'd be better off if He were dead. We've lived in ways that prove our distrust and disbelief in Him. We've chosen a path that leads to starvation and death, so that's what we deserve.

Despite all of this, God offers us a brand-new inheritance—one that has been reclaimed and redeemed by His Son, Jesus Christ, who came to earth and died for our sins. The bill was totaled up, and Christ died to settle that bill. After being crucified, He rose to life again, and He now beckons us home, having prepared a place for us. In the fullness of our sin, God responded with the fullness of His grace through Jesus Christ.

PART 3
IMMEDIATE ACTION

So he got up ...

Chapter 9

TIME TO GET UP

After graduating from high school, I went on a senior trip with my class to Dallas, Texas.[1] While we were there, I saw, for the first time, someone bungee jump. Bungee jumping was a relatively new phenomenon at the time, and at several hundred feet off the ground, this was one of the highest jumps in the country.

We watched as a guy got ready to make the leap with nothing but a cord strapped to his ankles. He dove off headfirst, and it was clear to me that the fellow students in my class were impressed.

In this moment I experienced another phenomenon known as *word vomit*. It's when a thought spews from your mouth before you can stop it. Here's what came out of my mouth: "I'd do that, but I'm not going to spend forty bucks on it."

I was trying to sound cool enough to bungee jump but too cool to actually spend the money. There was a little commotion behind

---

1   52,321 more candy bars, and it would have been Los Angeles. So close.

me, and one of the girls in my class pulled out a twenty-dollar bill and said, "Would this help?"

At this point, my back was kind of against the wall. A girl had called my bluff—in front of everyone. I could've said, "Well, I'm not going to spend twenty bucks on it either," but that wouldn't have gone over well. So without stopping to consider the fact that I don't like heights, I took the twenty and got in line.

As the crane lowered, I told myself, "It's not that high." But once the platform was at ground level and I stepped onboard, I was nervous. I smiled at my classmates, trying to put out a vibe of uncaring amusement, my best Luke Perry[2] imitation. But I was freaking out on the inside.

The guy who strapped the cord to my ankles did not inspire confidence. I'm pretty sure he was still wearing his 7-Eleven shirt from his other day job. The platform rose higher and higher until the crane finally lurched to a halt. I stepped to the edge, the tips of my Dr. Martens sandals sticking out over mere air. I could faintly hear my friends cheering me on, and then I made a horrible choice: I looked down. Suddenly, the full truth of my circumstances smacked me in the face: my friends were mere specks on a distant, unforgiving surface, and I was about to plummet toward them with nothing strapped to my body but a glorified rubber band that had been attached to me by a man who—for all I know—had been slinging Slurpees a few hours ago.

I had a white-knuckled death grip on the pole attached to the platform. Overcome with paralyzing fear, I turned to the crane

---

2   Don't question my choice of Luke Perry here. It was 1994.

operator and said, "I can't do it. I just can't do it!" But then a thought struck me, and I said, "Would you just give me a shove?"

Apparently I wasn't the first boy too scared to jump but too embarrassed to go down, because the worker replied, "Well, we're not legally allowed to push someone off."

Frustrated with this reply—*Thanks for being such a rule follower, Mr. 7-Eleven*—I said to him, "Do you have any other ideas for me?"

"Well, sometimes it works if you just close your eyes and fall," he said, adding, "Anybody can do that."

Well, fine, I thought, mustering some courage. *That sounds all right. I can do that. I can fall.*

So I stepped to the edge, closed my eyes, and I'm proud to say that … well, I didn't so much as bungee jump, I bungee *fell* that day, is what I did.

It's one thing to say what you are going to do, but it's another thing to do it. Action is where a lot of us get stuck. We know what needs to be done, we have stepped out onto the platform, but we just can't move. It's one thing to have the awakening and even to be honest about what we need to do. It's another thing entirely to take the leap.

Maybe this is a helpful picture: Think of AHA as a door that swings on three hinges. The first hinge is *a sudden awakening*. The second hinge is *brutal honesty*. The third and final hinge is *immediate action*. In Luke 15:20 we read a simple phrase that changed the story of the Prodigal Son. Jesus simply said, "So he got up …"

The Prodigal Son took immediate action. He recognized that it was time to get up. It was time to do something. And unless our story reads, "So he got up," or "So she got up," then nothing really changes. This is where AHA stalls out for so many of us. We have an awakening moment, we even find the strength to be brutally honest, but we never get around to actually doing anything different. We spend much of our lives stuck between honesty and action.

So He Got Up ... from the Couch

An example of what this looks like that most of us can relate to is in the area of diet and exercise.

First, there is a sudden awakening ...

Something happens, and you awaken to your current condition.

You put on the jeans from last year but can't get them buttoned.

You go outside to play catch with your kids and keep getting a side ache from too much physical exertion.

You sit down to watch TV, but when SportsCenter is over, you spend the next hour watching the WNBA because you lack the energy and stamina to walk across the room and get the remote control.

A buddy of mine told me about his sudden awakening in the area of physical exercise. One morning when he stepped out of the shower, his wife took one look at him and laughed out loud.

For me the moment came when I was at Starbucks getting my grande vanilla Frappuccino ... with no whip, I might add. As I was paying for my drink, a coin fell out of my pocket and landed on the floor. Instead of immediately bending over to pick it up, I looked down to see how much the coin was worth. Because if it were a penny, bending over to pick it up wouldn't be worth it; that would be too much work. If it were a quarter ... Well, that would be worth the intense physical exertion required to bend over. When I looked down and saw it was a nickel, I stood there for ten seconds debating if it was worth it. That was an awakening for me.

Next comes brutal honesty ...

You tell yourself the hard truth about yourself. You step on the scale, which takes a great deal of courage. You acknowledge the reality of the situation. No more denying or minimizing—now you know the truth. You step out of the shower and look at yourself in the mirror … and then look at the side view. Brutal.

You assess your diet and eating habits honestly and begin writing down how many calories you consume throughout the day. You add them up and tell yourself the truth. You go to the doctor and let her run a series of tests, and then you sit down and go over the results.

Now it's time for immediate action ...

You've had the awakening and the brutal honesty, but the real question is this: When your alarm goes off at 5:30 a.m., and you know the P90X guy, Tony Horton, is gonna yell at you[3] for the next forty minutes, what do you do? When the alarm goes off, and you know Denise Austin—with her bubbly personality and sweet smile (that you'd like to smack off her face)—is waiting for you, what are you going to do?

Will you get up?

---

3 I can't prove it but I am certain there is a direct correlation between how annoying a person is and how effective they are as a trainer. Need more evidence? Denise Austin, Jillian Michaels, Billy Blanks, Susan Powter ("Stop the Insanity!"), and Richard Simmons. I rest my case.

Will you take action?

Or will you just hit the snooze button and go back to sleep?

You've had the awakening and the brutal honesty, and now you need to change your eating habits. What are you going to do when you sit down at the restaurant and there's a two-for-one special going for mozzarella sticks or Southwestern egg rolls? It would be poor stewardship not to take advantage of this deal! Surely this deal is God giving you one last meal as a way to celebrate the choice you've made to eat better.

Opportunity to Act

Sadly, knowing we need to change doesn't always amount to change itself. I recently read an article that began with the following paragraph:

> Change or Die. What if you were given that choice? … What if a well-informed, trusted authority figure said you had to make difficult and enduring changes in the way you think and act? If you didn't, your time would end soon—a lot sooner than it had to. Could you change when change really mattered? When it mattered most?[4]

According to the article, the odds are nine to one against you changing—even in the face of certain death. The author based that

---

4   Alan Deutschman, "Change or Die," *Fast Company*, May 1, 2005, http://www.fastcompany.com/52717/change-or-die.

statistic on a well-known study by Dr. Edward Miller, former CEO of the hospital at Johns Hopkins University and former dean of the medical school there. Dr. Miller studied patients whose heart disease was so severe they had to undergo bypass surgery—a traumatic and expensive procedure that can cost more than $100,000 if complications arise. About 600,000 people have bypasses every year in the United States, and 1.3 million heart patients have angioplasties. These procedures provide a real chance for change for the patients. Because of the surgeries, they can now, through lifestyle changes, stave off pain and even death, if they're willing to act on the opportunity.

In our lives, if a sudden awakening calls attention to our heart disease, I hope we realize something is wrong. Following that, we have to allow brutal honesty to do its work in our hearts—essentially bypassing the lies we've believed or told ourselves.

Then we, like the heart patients, have an opportunity to act. Put another way, awakening happens to us, honesty happens in us, but nothing really changes unless action comes out of us.

But according to Dr. Miller's research, the change rarely takes place:

> If you look at people after coronary-artery bypass grafting two years later, 90 percent of them have not changed their lifestyle. And that's been studied over and over and over again. And so we're missing some link in there. Even though they know they have a very bad disease and they know they should change their lifestyle, for whatever reason, they can't.

Confusing Feelings for Action

I've learned that sometimes we get stuck between honesty and action because we trick ourselves into believing that because we *feel* different, we're actually *doing* something different. This is true despite the fact that we have yet to do anything. We mistake our conviction for real change. So we live with good intentions and strong convictions, but we never actually get around to leaving the pigpen.

Conviction is always an invitation to action. However, when convicted hearts don't lead to changed lives, there are some consistent side effects.

These side effects can also serve as symptoms or warnings that action needs to be taken.

An underlying sense of fatigue and frustration

A sudden awakening is an invitation to align your life with what's happening in your heart. When you don't take action that aligns your life with your heart, your life begins to violate your heart. From my own personal experience and from listening to the stories of others, I have learned that when actions violate convictions, a general sense of fatigue and frustration begins to mark one's life.

It's exhausting trying to live in a way that violates your heart. It leaves you constantly drained. The American Heart Association says to relieve stress: "Examine your values and live by them. The more your actions reflect your beliefs, the better you will feel ..."[5] Even

---

5   "How to Manage Your Stress," *USA Today*, March 7, 2001, http://usatoday30
     .usatoday.com/news/health/2001-03-07-stress-tips.htm.

secular health experts agree that we generally feel worse when our actions don't line up with our beliefs and values.

Imagine you wake up one day and turn on the local news. You are reminded that there is a marathon happening in town and you decide to run it. You haven't been training for this race, because you only just decided to run it this very day of the race.

What's going to happen?

You're not going to finish the race. Instead you're going to be in a lot of pain. Why? Your body would be violating your heart—and you hadn't trained for the race in advance. When our actions violate our heart, it leads to inevitable fatigue and frustration. It won't go away until you align your action with the awakening of your heart.

Unidentified tension in significant relationships

When you know what you need to do but have yet to do anything, it's only a matter of time before your frustration with yourself spills over onto others. If your life isn't aligned with your convictions, you become a hard person to live with.

Typically this shows up as a critical spirit. By their overt criticisms, an overly critical person reveals that there are things about themselves they know need to be addressed.

Sometimes this shows up in relationships when a person gets overly defensive. A person who feels guilty because they haven't taken action in areas of conviction tends to be overly sensitive and defensive, especially about things related to those areas of conviction where they have yet to take action.

When you put off taking action, it can cause you to treat other people with a "what's that supposed to mean?" attitude. That outward defensiveness often comes from an inner conviction that hasn't been acted upon.

Undirected anger

When there is an awakening without action, it always leads to guilt. You feel guilty that you aren't living your life in a way that is consistent with your convictions. Guilt almost always surfaces in anger. Anger, of course, is a secondary response.

I talk with people who say they struggle with a general sense of anger. It's not that they're angry toward a certain person or about a specific situation; they just feel angry. They try to dismiss it. They say, "Well, that's just the way I am ... I'm just wired that way."

If that describes you at all, then let me ask you a question. Don't get mad at me, but is it possible that the reason you can't identify why you're upset is because you're actually angry with yourself? Perhaps you feel guilty because you've been awakened to something but haven't done anything about it, in which case, it was only a matter of time before anger began to surface.

Where We Get Stuck

Immediate action may be where most of us get stuck, but it's important to recognize that without action, the story never changes. I want you to see a connection between these two phrases in Luke 15:

He came to his senses ... (v. 17)

So he got up ... (v. 20)

Without verse 20, verse 17 doesn't really matter.

"So he got up …" It sounds so simple, but it's easy to miss. If he doesn't get up, if he just stays in the pigpen living in brokenness, then really, who cares?

Michael Novak is a Catholic philosopher who makes the point that until there is action, our beliefs and convictions aren't genuine. He basically describes three different levels of belief.

First we have *public beliefs*. Public beliefs are beliefs we present to others, beliefs we try to get other people to think we believe, but which we don't really believe. So we will talk about our family, our marriage, or our finances in a way that isn't actually real—we just want people to think these are our convictions.

We also have *private beliefs*. Novak explains that private beliefs are the beliefs we have that we sincerely believe. We genuinely *believe* that we believe them. But when those beliefs are tested, we discover we don't *really* believe.

Lastly we have what Novak calls *core beliefs*. These are ultimately our only true beliefs, because they are beliefs backed up by reality. So it's not just something we say; it's not just something we feel; core beliefs actually define how we live. Our core convictions are determined by the actions we take.

Don't tell me about your beliefs and convictions; get up and show me.

Don't tell me you believe in spiritually influencing your children; get up, walk into their bedrooms, kneel beside their beds, and pray for them.

Don't tell me you love your wife; turn off SportsCenter, get off the couch, and take her out on a date. A real date. No, running to

Target to pick up a few things doesn't count as a date. I know because I tried … once.

Don't tell me you care about the poor; go serve at your local soup kitchen or log onto the Compassion International website and sponsor a child.

Your convictions aren't really worth anything until you take action.

Your Story Must Change

If the Prodigal Son had come to his senses but had never gotten up, then the story wouldn't have changed. If you're stuck between verses 17 and 20, then it's time to get up.

I talked to a husband this past week who told me his wife had just left him. For the first time he was clearly seeing some things he hadn't seen before. In the past he'd been proud and defensive and had blamed her for everything. Now he realized he'd put his work first, and he'd been putting his own needs ahead of hers and acting selfishly and pridefully.

When she left him, it was an awakening in his life that forced him to be honest and repentant.

Here's the question I asked him: "Okay, so what's the plan?"

"No, you don't understand," he said. "It's … um … well, it's complicated."

"No, you don't understand," I replied. "It may not be easy, but it's simple."

It's not easy to get up. I get that. But it is simple. Sometimes we have this complicated mess, and we want to address the complicated mess with a complicated plan, but really the truth is as simple as, "So he got up." Again, I'm not saying it's easy. The journey home would have been difficult. It would not have been easy to make that journey from the Distant Country on an empty stomach, but he gets up and goes.

So I know the journey won't be easy for this husband, but I am praying that the next part of his story reads, "So he got up."

A woman came to church who had not been close to God for a long time. Life in the Distant Country had taken its toll. Her past is full of pain, and she honestly doesn't have much hope for the future. She's been a closet alcoholic for years, which she's tried to keep a secret. She's finally being honest with herself about what her life has become. What she needs to do next won't be easy, but it isn't complicated. My prayer is that the next part of her story would read, "So she got up."

A man in his early twenties deleted the history on his computer. He promised himself, "Never again." He has lived with guilt and regret over his sin for years. He's had a few awakening moments, and he's been honest with how out of control his lust has become, but he's never really done anything to change it. When he caught me after a church service, he shook my hand and then leaned in close to me to say, in a low voice, "I've never told this to anyone before, but I really do need help." Now that he's confessed it, I'm hoping the next part of his story reads, "So he got up."

My question for you is: When are you going to get up?

When are you going to say to a friend, "Look, I've been able to keep it a secret, but I have a drinking problem, and I need help, because things are starting to spin out of control."

When are you going to end the relationship you *know* God wants you to end?

When are you going to be generous the way you know God has called you to be generous?

When are you going to make amends with the parents you've wounded?

When are you going to join a Bible study group for the first time in your life?

When are you going to start spiritually leading your family?

When are you going to talk to one of your coworkers about your faith?

When are you going to do something real about all the social-justice causes you post about online?

When are you going to invite your neighbor to church?

When is verse 20 going to be a part of your story?

It's time to get up.

Chapter 10

PASSIVITY—I'M SURE EVERYTHING WILL WORK ITSELF OUT

I'm sure you've seen the problems Southern California has with wild fires. When the conditions are dry and windy, a fire can spread quickly. When I lived in Southern California, we had ash falling from the sky like gray snow and landing in our yard several times. In fact, only a few months after we moved away, a fire actually spread to the hills directly behind our old house. When the national news reported on the fires, they showed pictures of our old neighborhood.

Not long after we moved away, there was a severe firestorm in Southern California that claimed some two dozen lives before it was finally put out. An article about the incident from *USA Today* carried this headline: "Hesitation Is a Fatal Mistake as California Firestorm Closes In."[6]

The article quoted Sergeant Conrad Grayson, who was frustrated that people were not acting with a greater sense of urgency. He said, "We're begging people to leave, and they don't take us seriously. They want to pack some clothes, or fight [the fire] in the backyard with a garden hose.... If people don't move fast, they're going to become charcoal briquettes."

Jon Smalldridge told of frantically warning his neighbors only to have some disregard him or respond too casually. He told of those who tried to save their televisions and computers before escaping. He said, "They looked like they were packing for a trip. The ones who listened to me and left the area, lived. The ones who didn't, died."

What is it that keeps us from acting with a greater sense of urgency? Instead of being aggressive, it seems more natural for us to respond passively. Even when the fire threatens and much is at stake, instead of acting, we tend to have an "I'm sure everything will work itself out" attitude.

The Prodigal Son didn't just hope his luck would change. He didn't wait for the famine to end and the economy to turn around. He came up with a plan of action. He said to himself, "I will set out and go back to my father and say to him ..." (Luke 15:18). That's the opposite of saying, "I will sit down, stay here, and hope for the best."

---

6   Scott Bowles, "Hesitation Is a Fatal Mistake as California Firestorm Closes In," *USA Today*, October 30, 2003, http://usatoday30.usatoday.com/news /nation/2003-10-30-fires-usat_x.htm.

We Love to *Watch* Action

It's an interesting irony about us as a society—we love action, but we would rather watch it than live it. We'll sit on the couch and order a pizza while we watch gourmet-cooking shows. We'll watch a home-improvement network for hours, and then get ourselves a drink from a leaky faucet. We will watch the contestants on *The Biggest Loser* push themselves until they are completely exhausted, but when it's over, we don't want to get out of the La-Z-Boy to get the remote control sitting across the room.

A passive response seems to be especially prevalent in men. Men love action movies. In fact, men, I want to test your manliness right now. Okay, that sounded awkward, but you know what I mean. I'll give you a quote, and you name the action movie from which it came:

> "Fight and you may die. Run and you'll live—at least a while. And dying in your beds many years from now, would you be willing to trade *all* the days—from this day to that—for one chance, just one chance, to come back here and tell our enemies that they may take our lives, but they'll never take our freedom!"[7] (HINT: Go back and read this with a Scottish accent.)

> "I don't know who you are. I don't know what you want. If you are looking for ransom, I can tell you

---

7   *Braveheart*

I don't have money. But what I do have are a very particular set of skills; skills I have acquired over a very long career. Skills that make me a nightmare for people like you."[8]

"The worst thing that happened to you, that can happen to any fighter: you got civilized."[9]

"What we do in life echoes in eternity."[10]

We love to *watch* action, right?

Don't tell my wife this, but I secretly watch UFC fights Sunday nights after a long weekend of preaching. When we men witness that kind of action, something comes alive in us. We find inspiration in the fighter who refuses to quit, the embattled soldier who rushes the enemy, or the athlete who rallies the team against all odds.

When the movie ends, however, what do we do?

Instead of fighting for our wives' honor, we just stand there and let our kids walk all over them.

Instead of being passionate about our marriage, we get passionate about sports.

Instead of fighting against temptation, we tap out and say it's too much.

-----

8   *Taken*
9   *Rocky III*
10 *Gladiator*

Instead of getting up, we recline in our La-Z-Boys and flip through our two hundred channels.

Passivity could be accurately described as the first sin we inherited from Adam. It may even be fair to say the first human sin wasn't eating the fruit; it was passivity. Remember when Eve took the fruit in the garden of Eden? What was Adam doing? Well, according to Genesis 3:6, Adam was right there with her.

He said nothing.

He did nothing.

He just stood there.

The Price of Passivity

Scripture gives us an unfortunate snapshot of passivity and its consequences in 1 Samuel. Eli served the Lord in the tabernacle as a priest and judge over Israel. He had two sons, Hophni and Phinehas, and they were also priests. But in chapter 2 verse 12, we read:

> Eli's sons were scoundrels; they had no regard for
> the LORD.

It's not that Hophni and Phinehas quit going to church even though they were the pastors, which has crossed my mind a time or two. We read that they stole money from the offering; they literally stole from God. They kept and ate the sacrifices meant for God. As if this weren't bad enough, they also slept with the women who served outside the sanctuary. They had *no* regard for the Lord.

If you're not familiar with the story, it's easy to assume Eli probably didn't know what was happening; otherwise he'd have put a stop to it, right? But Eli was aware of the situation. He knew what his sons were doing. *The Message* paraphrases 1 Samuel 2:22–25 this way:

> By this time Eli was very old. He kept getting reports on how his sons were ripping off the people and sleeping with the women who helped out at the sanctuary.

So there was this priest and father who heard bad reports coming in. Those reports were an awakening moment for him. People spoke the truth to him about his sons, and he experienced brutal honesty. It was time for Eli to take action.

"Eli took them to task," *The Message* says next. We hear that and think, *Finally, a little tough love, a little accountability for his sons. It's time to remove his boys as priests and put the fear of the Lord in them.*

But it goes on. Eli said to his boys:

> What's going on here? Why are you doing these things? I hear story after story of your corrupt and evil carrying on. Oh, my sons, this is not right! These are terrible reports I'm getting, stories spreading right and left among God's people! If you sin against another person, there's help— God's help. But if you sin against God, who is around to help?

That's all the action he took. He gave them a good talkin' to. That's what he did. He is what Dr. Phil calls a "threatening parent." A parent who says, "Well, next time …" or "If you do that again …" or "This time I mean it …" Eli said a lot of words but no action took place.

Scripture essentially says that Eli did nothing to stop them.

Even though he was a judge in the land, he didn't hand down a sentence or force them to make things right with others. Even though he was a priest in the temple's service, he didn't remove them from their posts to uphold the credibility of the priesthood.

Choosing Easy Over God

Scripture gives us a clue as to why Eli was so passive. It's easy to miss, but it's significant in understanding why we so often choose passivity over action.

In 1 Samuel 2:29, God asked Eli:

Why do you honor your sons more than me?

The Message says it this way:

Why do you treat your sons better than me?

When God used others to warn Eli about his sons, Eli did nothing, and in doing nothing, he chose his sons over God.

Don't miss this: *our passive approach to the action God has called us to take shows that we are honoring something more than Him.*

He convicts you about a dating relationship—but you don't do anything. Why? Because you honor your significant other more than you honor God.

He convicts you about lust—but you don't take any action, and in doing nothing, you honor your desires more than God.

He convicts you about being generous, but you still haven't started to give. Why? Because you honor your money more than you honor God.

He convicts you to be a spiritual leader, but you come home from work and spend the evening watching TV. Why? Because you honor sports more than God.

Passivity reveals that we've chosen something or someone over God.

But even in disobedience, God sent a messenger to warn Eli of impending consequences. In 1 Samuel 3:11–14, this is what God tells Eli:

> Listen carefully. I'm getting ready to do something in Israel that is going to shake everyone up and get their attention. The time has come for me to bring down on Eli's family everything I warned him of, every last word of it. I'm letting him know that the time's up. I'm bringing judgment on his family for good. He knew what was going on, that his sons were desecrating God's name and God's place, and he did nothing to stop them. This is my sentence on the family of Eli: The evil of Eli's family can never be wiped out by sacrifice or offering. (MSG)

Here, Eli had another chance to act, to come before the Lord in repentance and seek His mercy. How would the story have changed if at this point we read, "So he got up"? But Eli didn't get up. Here's his response:

> He is GOD. Let him do whatever he thinks best.
> (1 Sam. 3:18 MSG)

Eli had just found out that his family and any future generations in his family were going to experience long-term consequences and his response was, "Well, God is God. Let Him do what He thinks is best." That may sound superspiritual, like Eli was being submissive to the will of God. But he wasn't being submissive; he was being passive.

Remember, Eli was a priest. He should have been willing to go before the Lord in brokenness and stand and act on behalf of his family. Instead he sat back and said, "Whatever God wants. That's fine by me." What God wants for you to do, Eli, is to get up and fight for your family and for justice! Eli, God wants you to stand up for His honor in His house and choose Him over your sons! What God wants is for you to stop talking and actually do something!

Compare Eli to a man named Nehemiah. He led God's people in an effort to rebuild the walls of Jerusalem. It reached a point where the work seemed to be too much and the opposition seemed too overwhelming. But Nehemiah called the men of Israel to be men of action. He essentially challenged them by asking, "Did you think this was going to be easy? Did you think the wall was going to just build itself?" And then he said to them, "Pick up a sword and fight."

Men, when will you put down the remote control, choose God, and stand up for your family? Put down the cell phone, pick up a sword, and fight for your marriage. Put down the PlayStation controller, put down the 9 iron, put down the iPad, and fight for *something*. It may even be time to put down this book. Maybe you've heard enough; stop reading, watching, talking, and playing—*it's time for action.*

Shortcut to the Pigpen

Eli wasn't the only passive one in this story. Eli's sons grew up with a sense of entitlement. They knew from the day they were born that they'd be priests—an honored position in Israel's hierarchy. The good life had been handed to them; they didn't have to *earn* their positions of honor.

So as they grew up pampered and well taken care of, they ended up with a very entitled outlook on life, which can often lead to passivity. And we read that these sons "had no regard for the LORD." They just didn't care. They did as they pleased and expected everything to work out. This kind of entitled passivity says, "Who cares? I'll end up with the things I want whether or not I try." "It doesn't matter if I do anything, because one way or another, it'll work out."

I want you to carefully read the line below to see if you recognize it:

Up, up, down, down, left, right, left, right, B, A, start.

Can you identify this code?

It's a cheat code from the Nintendo[11] game *Contra*, which was a favorite game of mine growing up. I am told that it works on several other games as well. I loved *Contra*, but I could never beat it.

One day my friend Brian came over, and we were playing *Contra* when he blew my mind. When the game turned on, he entered that cheat code on the controller—up, up, down, down, left, right, left, right, B, A, start—and he got thirty free lives. Through some coercion, he gave the cheat code to me to use as well, and it changed the way I played. From then on, I didn't even have to try hard. I just assumed everything would work out because I had the cheat code.

Passivity looks for shortcuts, for cheats, for a way around, while immediate action moves directly. Passivity looks for the path of least resistance—the wide path. Immediate action looks for the path of righteousness—the narrow one.

Passivity wants to cheat. Action wants to change.

Passivity says, "Everything will work itself out." Action says, "This is going to take some work."

Passivity says, "What's the least I can get away with?" Action says, "What needs to be done?"

The Prodigal Son finally did the hard thing. He took action. He rejected passivity, made a game plan, and followed through. Action can be that simple and that difficult. Let's be honest: it's not easy to get up and walk home when you've been picked up and carried your whole life.

---

11 You can separate generations by their gaming systems. I go back to Nintendo, the greatest of all consoles. In my opinion it's not a real gaming system if you don't have to blow on the cartridge before it will work.

Obey Anyway

So maybe you're reading this chapter and agreeing with me. You see some passivity in your life and know you need to change. Maybe you've been entitled, or maybe you've not been a man or woman of action. At the same time, you might be reading this and thinking, *I agree with you, but I just don't feel like doing anything about it.*

I know how you feel.

It may sound a little cold, or perhaps a bit trite; however, the truth is we need to obey God even when we don't feel like it. When we obey God without the motivation to do so, our feelings will eventually catch up with our actions.

I remember learning this lesson when we lived in California. One thing that stressed me out there was the traffic. I hated sitting in traffic. One day I was sitting in a line of cars not going anywhere, riding the bumper of the car in front of me. I honked my horn, hoping that somebody miles up the road would hear it and decide to go a little faster. I kept switching lanes, trying to move ahead a few extra feet, and I was completely stressed out.

I knew this wasn't what God wanted for me. He wanted me to be at peace. I didn't feel at peace, so I decided to fake it and see what would happen. I thought to myself, *I'm not a man at peace, but if I was, what would I do?*

Well, for starters, I would back off the car in front of me. I would quit honking my horn, and I wouldn't switch lanes. A man at peace would probably put in a sermon or worship CD. So I stuck in a worship CD. A man at peace would probably sing along with this CD, so I started to sing. A man at peace would smile, so I forced myself to smile. A man at peace might wave at somebody, so I waved. I thought a man at peace would probably let someone else in front of him. But it's hard to say for sure, so I didn't go ahead with that one.

I don't know when it happened, but at some point I began to feel at peace. You see, our attitudes and emotions can catch up with our actions. We are called to be obedient even when we don't feel like it.

Look back at your game plan for the changes you need to make. You've probably made the list before, whether on paper or in your mind, and you know what they are. Identify the first step, just like the Prodigal Son did when he pointed out, "I will go home and say to my father ..." He knew what he needed to do, and he carried it out. Find your first step and act on it now, whether or not you want to. And you may find that along the road, with God's help, actions that at first seem artificial can become authentic.

Chapter 11

PROCRASTINATION—I'LL GET TO IT LATER

[INTRO NEEDED HERE]

This note has been at the top of this chapter for weeks now. Whenever I work on a book, I always want to make sure the chapters open with a clear teaching, interesting story, or intriguing illustration. The last thing I want to do is open with a definition of the word *procrastination* for you.[1] No, you deserve more. But those stories don't always come easily, so sometimes when I'm writing, I just make a note like above so I can move on and come back to it later.

Unfortunately, the final version of this manuscript has to go to the publisher tomorrow, and I still don't have an opener for this chapter. I just kept assuming I would get to it, and here we

---

1 Dictionary.com defines *procrastination* as "the act or habit of procrastinating, or putting off or delaying, especially something requiring immediate attention."

are. Now you're reading this book, and I'm still short an introduction. You're experiencing the consequences of my procrastination. *My bad.*

You see, that's the thing about telling ourselves, "I'll get to it later." If we tell ourselves that enough, the urgency evaporates, and our procrastination has consequences.

The Prodigal Son's action was immediate. The word *so* in the phrase "So he got up ..." indicates a quick response. It's best to understand verses 17 through 20 as one movement. It's a continuation. He said, "Here's what I'm going to do ..." and then he got up and did it. After having an awakening and an honest moment, we often sit in the pigpen trying to come up with a plan or promising ourselves that—sometime soon—we will take action. But the Bible doesn't say of the Prodigal Son: "The next day he got up ..." or "After some time passed ..." or "When the weather was good for traveling ..." It says, "So he got up." He took action immediately.

Procrastination is one of the chief tools Satan uses to prevent AHA from happening in your life. He knows that if you put off taking action long enough, you will soon go back to sleep. And here's why procrastination is so effective: Even though we are still sitting in the pigpen, we feel as though we've done something. It lets us off the hook because we're not saying, "No;" we're just saying, "Not right now." We're not turning the alarm off; we're just hitting the snooze button. So we're able to close our eyes and go back to sleep, because we have every intention of getting up—just not yet.

There are a few reasons why we have this proclivity toward procrastination:

We want to put off the pain

Why do they make workout commercials where everyone appears happy and relaxed? You've seen those commercials, haven't you? A sweatless woman walks on a treadmill while a man easily works the weight machine. Both are smiling. Both look calm, as though working out is a fun way to kill time and requires no exertion.

We think, *Just ten minutes a day and I'll have abs like her*, or, *In just a couple of months I'll smile fifteen pounds away.* But when you go to the gym, what are people doing? They're grunting and groaning, straining with determination, contorting their faces into comically embarrassing expressions. It's never as easy as they make it look in the commercial, right? If it were pain-free, we would act. Most of us don't want to act, because we don't want the pain.

So we put it off.

We put off the workouts, because we don't want sore muscles.

We put off living within our means, because we don't want to cut back on our lifestyle.

We put off the hard conversation, because we don't want awkward tension.

We put off getting help, because we don't want to feel vulnerable.

We put off asking for forgiveness, because we don't want to embarrass ourselves.

The Prodigal Son knew how hard making the trip back home was going to be. He knew how painful it would be to see the disappointment in his father's eyes. He knew how humbling it would be to feel the judgment and condemnation from his older brother. He knew it would be painful, shaming, and difficult. Waiting wasn't going to make it any easier. In fact, the longer he put off action, the more difficult it would become.

So he got up.

We want to prolong the pleasure

The truth is that spending money on wild living in the Distant Country sounds fun. We sometimes like to talk and act like sin isn't fun ... like it doesn't ever feel good ... or bring any happiness. The truth is that often it does. Ultimately, it doesn't last and brings much greater pain. But in the moment it's fun. There's a reason some people sleep around, get hammered on weekends, or experiment with drugs. They experience earthly pleasure. They may say, "It makes me feel good," or "It helps me blow off some steam," or "I love how it feels to be wanted by someone."

Even though we know these kinds of choices lead to the pigpen, we still think we have time to enjoy them. Until the famine comes, we tend to put off any action, believing we can live it up a while longer without multiplying our consequences.

Unfortunately, this kind of procrastination often has the opposite effect. Let's say the Prodigal Son lived in our culture today. He would have run out of money, but then, in order to prolong the pleasure, he would have continued his wild living by racking up credit-card debt. How much more would that have complicated his story? How much worse would it have been for the son to arrive home with looming debt? Picture him saying, "Father, I've sinned against heaven and against you. I have no money, and by the way, some creditors are coming, and I owe twice what my inheritance was worth." The longer we try to prolong the pleasure, the greater the pain will be.

I recently read an article about professional athletes and how they deal with retirement. Most of us will work at least forty years, then retire for twenty or so. Professional athletes work for ten or fifteen years, if they're lucky, and retire for sixty. However, so many of these athletes live extravagant lifestyles during their careers that catch up with them once they retire. Instead of cutting back and making changes, they try to prolong the pleasure.

One player I read about is now basically broke. His original contract to play amounted to over one hundred million dollars, and now he's broke. He owes almost a million dollars to his personal jeweler. And he will get a deferred payment in two decades for $30 million in sponsorships, which complicates it further. He's broke now, but in twenty years, he'll collect a cool $30 million. So he's able to borrow now against a payment he won't receive for a while. As a result he continues to spend and accumulate debt. He's prolonging the pleasure, but the later pain will be that much greater.

We want to plan it to perfection

Notice that the Prodigal Son's plan of action wasn't complicated. It was pretty simple. Get up, go home, and talk to his father. That was his simple plan of action. He didn't plan a pit stop to get cleaned up. He didn't work up a way to make back a little bit of money so he wasn't going home broke. He didn't complicate the plan with any unnecessary steps.

Keeping it simple can be hard, but when you try to tie up every possible loose end, you end up frustrated and convinced you need to work harder. Sometimes we just need a simple plan of action—even if it's imperfect.

Recently, a church my buddy pastors was going through a series on relationships, and they asked me to come out and preach on the topic of sexual intimacy.

That's kind of a sensitive topic—especially as a guest speaker.

Before the trip I talked to my wife, saying, "You know, I wonder why they gave me this topic. Of all the topics, why'd they give me this one for this series?"

My wife said, "Sometimes they've got to call in the experts."[2]

So I went to preach about sexual intimacy. Afterward, a young college student who was probably twenty-one years old came forward to talk to me. I often see this kind of guy come forward when sex is addressed in church. Most of them have grown up in the church and either struggle with porn or have a girlfriend and have a hard time abstaining.

He walked up to me and said, "Here is my challenge. I've been dating this girl for four years, and we love each other and we're going to get married. We've been struggling to remain pure, and we even talked about getting married—though my folks would flip out if we did that before finishing grad school. We've made a commitment to start obeying God in this area of our lives. But I just don't know. I just …" He trailed off and finally said, "I don't know how we're going to do this. I don't know what we're going to do."

---

2   I made that up. She didn't say that, but that's what I pretended to hear.

I said, "Well, look. Here are your options. You're not going to like either one of them. Option number one: you can say that for the next two or three years you are going to be patient and pure, that as boyfriend and girlfriend you'll be committed to doing things God's way. But I'm going to tell you, you're going to have a really hard time with that. It's going to add a ton of pressure and guilt and blame to your relationship. It's going to be difficult."

I continued, "Your other option is to decide that you're going to get married and set a date for the summer, eight months from now. You know you want to get married. Yeah, Mom and Dad may not love that, but they'll be okay. And you might be poor at first, right? But that's fun. That's what ramen noodles are for. It's fun to be young and married and poor. And it'll be okay."

As we talked, I tried to imagine the rest of his scenario. His parents were probably lifelong Christians, and he had grown up going to every church function imaginable. He's known all along what God's Word says about sexual intimacy, yet for the last four years he's been in this intimate relationship. Still, he and his girlfriend really want to start over and make a commitment.

I had already assumed this false backstory, so I obviously hadn't minced words with him. I know what it's like to be in a dating relationship at that age, and guys need to hear it straight.

Then he said, "Well, I just became a Christian a couple of weeks ago, so all of this is new to me."

I tried not to let my eyes go wide at this, but I was floored. This newborn in Christ was experiencing AHA in this area of his life for the first time ever—and he was already jumping into action! As we talked some more, he clearly recognized that this wasn't going to be easy. But he ended our conversation with this: "I know I want to do what God wants me to do—no matter what that is."

He knew there was no way to perfect the plan. He knew his parents wouldn't necessarily agree with the decision. He knew it wouldn't be easy. He also knew what God wanted him to do. Even though the situation was complicated, the game plan was simple.

So what action do you need to take? You may be surprised how something as simple as making a phone call, scheduling an appointment, cutting up a credit card, or unfriending a Facebook friend can be a step toward your journey home.

Little Guy, Big Change

One of my favorite AHA stories in Scripture is found in Luke 19. Jesus was passing through Jericho, where a man named Zacchaeus lived. In Luke 19:2, the Bible says, "He was a chief tax collector and was wealthy." Maybe your version says, "He was very rich." The word used here for *wealthy* means "extreme wealth." We are talking the cultural equivalent of multiple vacation homes and a fleet of cars. He's in the top 1 percent of the 1 percenters.

We know Zacchaeus was really rich, but he was also really short. The Bible doesn't often give physical descriptions of people. When the Bible gives descriptions, I immediately get an image in my mind of who I would cast for that role. I was thinking Joe Pesci would be a good Zacchaeus, right? Pesci's this little guy known for having a high, annoying voice who dresses really well.

Picture Zacchaeus in this crowd. He was shorter than most, so elbows were flying near his face as all these rubberneckers jockeyed for a view of Jesus. Zacchaeus finally gave up trying to compete with the crowd and climbed up a sycamore tree. He was perched in the tree when Jesus arrived.

Here's what we read in Luke 19:5–7:

> When Jesus reached the spot, he looked up and said to him, "Zacchaeus, come down immediately. I must stay at your house today." So he came down at once and welcomed him gladly.
>
> All the people saw this and began to mutter.

The people realized that Jesus was going to go eat with Zacchaeus, the tax collector, and in verse 7, they began to mutter: "He has gone to be the guest of a sinner." The reason Zacchaeus was called a sinner here is not because having money is inherently bad. The problem was how he got his money in the first place.

Zacchaeus was a chief tax collector, which basically made him kind of the Bernie Madoff of his day, running a kind of ancient Ponzi scheme.

This is how it worked: Jewish tax collectors would go out on behalf of the Roman government—the occupying enemy—and they would take money from the Israelites—their own people. They would say to their people, "Taxes this year are $150." And they'd give one hundred dollars to the Romans and then pocket fifty dollars for themselves. This is how tax collectors grew wealthy. Each tax collector would then give a percentage of the fifty dollars they'd pocketed to the chief tax collector. That was Zacchaeus. He wasn't just a sinner; he sinned for a living. It was his job. It was what was on his business card: certified Sinner.

Proverbs 20:23 warns us, "The LORD detests differing weights, and dishonest scales do not please him." Proverbs 28:6 says, "Better the poor whose walk is blameless than the rich whose ways are perverse."

The bottom line is that from a biblical perspective, morality is more important than prosperity. God cares less about what you've got and more about how you got it and what you do with it. When someone hoarded money the way Zacchaeus did, people didn't want anything to do with him.

But when Jesus came along and said to Zacchaeus, "I'm gonna come eat at your house," Zacchaeus was thrilled. It was an honor for this rabbi to stop and eat with him. My guess is that Zacchaeus was used to eating well, but he was used to eating alone. The townspeople probably didn't like seeing him around, much less going to his house and being seen with him.

However, something happened during that meal that changed Zacchaeus's heart.

He had accumulated wealth, but he had also been searching; he had been trying to find some kind of satisfaction. Nothing had worked, but when he met Jesus, he said, "This is it! This is what I have been looking for." He had this sudden awakening because of his encounter with Jesus. He realized that what he was looking for wasn't something one can buy.

Zacchaeus also had to face some hard truths. The reality was that he'd turned his back on his own people and he couldn't blame anyone else. Some poor people had become even poorer because of his actions. Peasants had been forced to skip meals because of his greed. He had to look at his life honestly and take responsibility for it.

So this is what we read in Luke 19:8:

> Zacchaeus stood up and said to the Lord, "Look,
> Lord! Here and now I give half of my possessions
> to the poor, and if I have cheated anybody out of
> anything, I will pay back four times the amount."

In the wake of his startling realization and in the face of the honest truth, he took action. Can you imagine how this would've been a testimony to the people in the community?

Earlier in the chapter, the people were upset that Jesus was going to go eat with this sinner. What do you think they thought of Jesus after Zacchaeus came out and announced what he was going to do? They would have been amazed!

When our AHA experience finds its fulfillment in immediate action, Jesus is glorified. When those people saw Zacchaeus transformed, they knew it could only be because of Jesus. The same is true in our lives. Our friends have probably seen us struggle with making wise choices. When we experience AHA and it results in immediate action and life changes, they will recognize that it wasn't by our power or through our determination. It was because of Jesus.

Here's the phrase I want you to pay special attention to in the story of Zacchaeus. In verse 8, just before Zacchaeus announced his plan he said, "*Here and now* I give ..."

Here and now.

I'm not gonna wait until later. I'm not gonna wait until I reach a certain level. I'm not going to put this off. But *here and now* I'm going to be generous and pay back those I cheated.

That's your challenge today. Take action immediately. Let it start *here* and *now*.

Zacchaeus's story concludes this way in verse 9: "Jesus said to him, 'Today salvation has come to this house, because this man, too, is a son of Abraham. For the Son of Man came to seek and to save the lost.'"

I've been blessed to have heard and read many AHA stories over the years, and I've noticed that while they may differ in many ways, the way people tell them is very similar. In fact, after reading hundreds of stories, I was struck that most of them included a certain time and a certain place:

I was in my living room that afternoon …
We were at the church later that weekend …
I sat in my car early that morning …

We often remember the time and place, because in that moment, we stopped putting off change and allowed Jesus to change us in the here and now. This is what Jesus does. He changed the heart of Zacchaeus, and He can change our hearts as well. But it needs to start *here* and *now*.

Shakespeare said, "Tomorrow, and tomorrow, and tomorrow … have lighted fools / The way to dusty death."[3] When there is an awakening and you come to your senses and know something needs to be done and think to yourself, *Tomorrow I will* … or *Next week I'm going to* … That is not the Holy Sprit. The Holy Spirit does not procrastinate.

---

3   William Shakespeare, *Macbeth* (New York: New American Library, 1998), 90.

[CONCLUSION NEEDED HERE]

Your story of taking action would be the perfect ending to this chapter.

I'll get you started:

Here and now I …

Chapter 12

DEFEATISM—IT'S TOO LATE NOW

I got a call from a woman in our church whose elderly mother was dying of pancreatic cancer. Her mother, Paulette, didn't have much time left, days at the most. Hospice had been called in. The daughter told me Paulette had not been to church since she was a young girl. It had probably been somewhere around sixty years since she had spoken to a pastor. But Paulette wanted someone to talk to her about Jesus, so her daughter asked if I would come and talk to her mom. I said I'd be honored to do that and drove over to the house.

When I walked in the door and saw Paulette, the toll this horrible disease had taken was clear. Too weak to walk, she sat in a wheelchair. Her frail frame slouched forward. Her husband was there, in good health, and as soon as I walked in, he made it clear to me that he was not a Christian and had no intention of becoming one. He belonged to a different kind of faith altogether.

He smiled at me and said, "Give me thirty days and I'll convert you."

I liked him right away.

I followed him as he wheeled Paulette into the family room, and then he left us alone. I sat down next to her and began to tell her what the Bible teaches. I explained, "The Bible says that we've all sinned, Paulette."

That was hard to say to an elderly lady who was dying of pancreatic cancer, but I knew she already knew this. When someone wants to talk to a pastor days before their death, there are always some things that need to be made right.

So I said to Paulette, "I've sinned; you've sinned. The Bible says that the wages of our sin, the punishment that we deserve because of our sin, is death. But here is the great news. The Bible teaches that 'God so loved the world that He gave His only Son.' That if we put our trust in Him, we won't perish but we'll have eternal life. Jesus came to this earth and He died on a cross to forgive us of our sins. He took our punishment upon Himself. So when you put your trust in Jesus as Lord and Savior, you are forgiven. You can't save yourself. It doesn't matter how much good you do in this life. It's a free gift that comes from God through Jesus. In Him there is a fresh start, a new beginning, and the promise of eternal life."

Paulette began to cry.

She wasn't crying the emotional tears someone sheds when they finally come home after being in the Distant Country. She was disturbed by something I'd said. I wasn't sure what had triggered the response, so I asked her, "What are the tears for?"

Her head was bowed and her gaze low. "I just wish it wasn't too late for me," she said. "I've had my chances, but what can I do now? It's too late."

So many of us hear the gospel the way Paulette heard it that day. She heard that we've sinned and that God sent Jesus to die for us and to offer us a second chance, but somehow we add the condition that we need to accept this gift within a certain time frame before our bill in the Distant Country gets too high.

We see the mess we're in, and instead of taking action, we tell ourselves, "It's too late."

My kids are too old.

My marriage is too broken.

My friend is too angry.

My reputation is too far gone.

My debt is too overwhelming.

My addiction is too powerful.

My life is too messed up.

Life can reach a point when it feels like things have gone too far. There are too many broken pieces to put back together. I'm sure the Prodigal Son must have felt that way. His life was way past fixing. But eventually, he must have decided he didn't have anything to lose. He had no money left. He had no friends left. He had no more physical strength. He had no options. Sometimes rock bottom *is* the best place to be, because that's what it takes to experience AHA, though it doesn't have to be.

Thief on the Cross

If there was ever a man who must have thought it was too late, it was one of the men crucified next to Jesus. The Bible tells us in Matthew 27 that there were two criminals crucified on either side of Jesus. Scripture also says that they both mocked Him and said cruel things to Him. But something happened to one of the two criminals. He experienced AHA as he hung on that cross next to Jesus.

Luke also records what happened:

> One of the criminals on a cross began to shout insults at Jesus. "Aren't you the Christ? Then save yourself and us." But the other criminal stopped him and said, "You should fear God! You are getting the same punishment he is. We are punished justly, getting what we deserve for what we did. But this man has done nothing wrong." Then he said, "Jesus, remember me when you come into your kingdom." Jesus said to him, "I tell you the truth, today you will be with me in paradise." (Luke 23:39–43 NCV)

Do you see it? He had a sudden awakening. He saw who Jesus truly was. He was brutally honest as he admitted that he was getting what he deserved for his sin. Then he took action. He both defended Jesus and cried out to Him for help. With his dying breath, he asked God to save him. What made him think it wasn't too late? He was a convicted criminal dying for crimes he committed, and he had no time left to make things right, no chance to offer restitution to his victims.

I began to think about what he witnessed that would have made him think it wasn't too late to act. He would have listened as Jesus cried, "My God, my God, why have you forsaken me?" (Matt. 27:46).

Was that what changed him? The words Jesus cried are a direct quote from Psalm 22, a piece of literature more than a thousand years old that spoke of pierced hands and feet before the punishment of crucifixion had even been realized.

Why would Jesus feel forsaken and separated from God? Well, for the first time in His short life on earth, He didn't share perfect fellowship with His Father. Second Corinthians 5:21 explains, "God made him who had no sin to be sin for us, so that in him we might become the righteousness of God."

Read that again.

Jesus became sin.

He took upon Himself the sin of the world, and that separated Him from His Father. He was separated so that we could be reunited. Is this what transformed the thief that day? It's hard to say.

The thief would have also heard Jesus speak to Mary, His mother. She wasn't far from the cross with John, the disciple whom Jesus loved. Jesus spoke to her and John, saying, "Woman, here is your son … [John] here is your mother" That must have softened the thief's heart. Jesus was enduring the most excruciating pain imaginable, and in the midst of that, He thought of His mother. He wanted to see that she was taken care of and protected. What selfless love. Maybe that was the moment.

I'll tell you which moment I think it was. Surely what made the thief take action was the prayer that Jesus prayed on the cross. Jesus prayed for the soldiers who crucified Him. He didn't pray for their destruction. He didn't pray for them to be punished. He prayed that God would forgive them.

This thief was going through the same suffering Jesus was and at the hands of the same soldiers. He would have been filled with anger and rage toward those responsible. But Jesus said, "Father, forgive them."

What do you do with that kind of grace? I think it just wrecked that thief. His heart softened in that moment. Who was this man who spoke forgiveness for His own executioners?

Maybe, the thief must have thought, *it's not too late for me after all.*

Just the Right Time

Instinctively, I reached over and grabbed Paulette's hand.

At this point she wasn't the only one who was crying. I could feel tears rolling down my own face as I told her, "Oh no, no, no. It is just the right time. It is never too late with Jesus." In her family room, we prayed together. I led her in a prayer of repentance and confession. Afterward, even though she was still physically weak, she wanted to get baptized to express her new faith. It was a beautiful moment as she was baptized along with her daughter and her granddaughter. I was so inspired by Paulette. It takes a lot of courage to get to the end of the road, realize it's a dead end, and turn around.

The Prodigal Son reached his own dead end, but he was willing to act. "So he got up ..." He took action, but how would his speech be received when he got home? That question must have crossed his mind as he made the journey. He did what he could, but honestly, that wasn't much. He humbled himself and owned up to his mistakes, but would that be enough?

Many of us assume that our relationship with God is measured in this kind of quantitative calculation. So the word *enough* haunts many Christians. We look at our lives, tally up our rights and our wrongs, and are faced with the defeating truth: *we can never do enough*. We can't out-right our wrongs. Sure, we can make up for a few mistakes, but we can all look at our lives and admit that—in one way or another—we've done irreparable damage. There isn't enough time to make things right, so we end up doing nothing. The time for action has come and gone. So with our head bowed and eyes low, we say, "It's too late now."

Trying Only Makes It Worse

Last summer my family had the opportunity to house-sit for some friends of ours. House-sitting isn't normally something that sounds fun, but it was the heat of summer and these friends had an above-ground pool in their backyard. My kids were especially excited about this. We were ready to relax by the pool and cool off.

The first morning we were there, my wife said, "Hey, I think there may be a leak in their pool, because it looks like it's lost some water. I'm pretty sure the water level dropped during the night."

So I went out to investigate, and, sure enough, the water level was down around six or eight inches from what it had been the night before. I examined the exterior of the pool, but I couldn't find a leak. I realized that I was gonna have to get in there and find the leak. This meant I needed some swim goggles. The only goggles I could find were my son's green goggles that were so tight they cut the circulation off from the rest of my head, but they would have to do. They suctioned onto my face like two sea urchins, and I dove in and started looking for the leak. Sure enough, I found a small hole near the bottom of the pool that was about the size of a pencil eraser. Water was leaking out steadily, but it wasn't too bad, so I didn't feel a great sense of urgency to fix it.

That afternoon, I headed to the pool store. I explained the situation, and they sold me a round patch made of clear vinyl, along with a transparent adhesive like rubber cement. The pool guy said, "You smear this glue on the patch. You swim down to the spot. And you just press it gently against the edges of the hole, and that'll take care of it."

So I went back to our friends' house, smeared the glue on the patch, swam down to the leak, and gently pressed the patch against the hole.

Like they'd said, it wasn't a big deal.

But then the hole expanded.

One second I was plugging a leak the size of an eraser, and the next second, my hand was getting sucked through a vortex the size of a basketball. And this vortex was also sucking out eighteen thousand gallons of water, and it was all trying to get out at once. My brain panicked, telling my arm to pull back, but there was just too much water pushing down.

A thought struck me: *I'm gonna drown in my buddy's above-ground pool.* Desperate not to become someone else's sermon illustration, I pushed hard off the bottom of the pool and managed to climb out. Once out of the pool, something in my brain said, *Get towels.* So I grabbed towels and attempted to stuff them in the hole.

The hole ripped wider.

I ended up watching eighteen thousand gallons of water being dumped into my buddy's backyard.

I was thinking, *What just happened?*

I wish this story had some kind of happy ending, but it doesn't. In fact, I didn't even get a refund on the patch from the pool guys. My attempt was a complete failure. I single-handedly turned a small leak into a full-blown disaster.

Some of us have tried to patch things up before, and it hasn't ended well. We've acted with good intentions, but our attempts to fix our problems have only made them worse. We've tried to reconcile relationships, but it's always ended with wounding words and responses we regret. We've set boundaries and distanced ourselves from temptation, but the relapse seems unavoidable. We get back up, determined to do better, only to fall harder.

You may be reading this thinking, *I've tried to change, and it's never worked. It's too late.* But let me ask you a few questions:

When you tried to patch things up, did you try it your way or God's way?

When you made an attempt to start over, was it on your terms or God's?

When you last tried to act, were you brutally honest with yourself and God, or did you skip honesty and go straight from awakening to action?

When you tried to stick with it, was it on your own power or by the power of the Holy Spirit?

When you acted, was it motivated by guilt and shame or by the love and grace of Jesus?

It's Up to Me

Perhaps you remember, in 2010, watching Tiger Woods apologize for his affairs. He had his awakening—a 9 iron to the head usually does the job. He had his honesty—every magazine cover on the rack told the brutal truth. And for fifteen minutes, he laid out his plan of action, telling the world what he was going to do. In his interview, Tiger mentioned his Buddhist faith and the teachings of Buddhism were evident in his words. Buddhists have an eight-fold path, a religious walk that is based solely on an individual's performance. If you can live a good-enough life, or multiple lives, you can rack up enough points and reach enlightenment and Nirvana. And because it's all about being good enough, there is always a lot to do. You could hear that in Tiger's speech. He talked a lot about the actions he needed to take. Here are a few of the phrases he used:

I have a lot to atone for …
It's now up to me …
I have a long way to go …
I am the one who needs to change …
I need to make my behavior more respectful …
It's up to me …
I have a lot of work to do …

As I watched Tiger apologize, I thought a lot about the parable of the prodigal son. As Jesus told this parable, everyone in the first-century audience was probably thinking the same thing—his father is going to let him have it. The father is going to disown him and will likely refuse to acknowledge his presence. The Prodigal Son, like Tiger Woods, had a lot of work to do to atone for his sins. At the very least, that boy was going to be shoveling excrement until he paid his father back—with interest.

We read the son's action: "So he got up and went to his father ..."

But what action would the father take? A spirit of defeatism may be reasonable if it all depended on us. If we could only make things right through our actions, then, yeah, for a lot of us it is too late—*way too late*. A spirit of defeatism comes because we don't accurately take into account how the Father will respond when we come home.

Here's how Jesus tells it in Luke 15:

> But while he was still a long way off, his father saw him and was filled with compassion for him; he ran to his son, threw his arms around him and kissed him.
>
> The son said to him, "Father, I have sinned against heaven and against you. I am no longer worthy to be called your son."
>
> But the father said to his servants, "Quick! Bring the best robe and put it on him. Put a ring on his finger and sandals on his feet. Bring the fattened calf and kill it. Let's have a feast and celebrate.

For this son of mine was dead and is alive again; he
was lost and is found." So they began to celebrate.
(Luke 15:20–24)

There are two parts of this story that would have been especially shocking to first-century listeners. First, when the Prodigal
Son asked for his inheritance from his father while the father was
still alive. One Jewish scholar pointed out that for the son to ask
his father for his inheritance while the father was still alive was
equivalent to wishing the father were dead.

But even more shocking than the son's blatant disrespect and
coldhearted selfishness is the undeserved grace and extravagant love
the father showed when his son returned. The way Jesus described
the grace and love of the father was scandalous.

The son "was still a long way off" when the father went to him.
The father wasn't going to wait. Just like God doesn't wait for you
to make it home on your own. In fact, before you even thought
about taking action, He had already acted. The Bible says that while
we were still sinners, Christ died for us. While we were still in the
Distant Country feeding pig slop to pigs, He acted.

What truly made this moment shocking is this detail about
the father: he ran to his son. Culturally this just didn't happen. The
patriarch of a Jewish family didn't run. He would never hike up his
robes and take off running. It wasn't sophisticated. It wasn't refined.
It wasn't distinguished.

It's not too late, because the Father has made up lost ground.

Look again at how the father responded when he got to his son.
Jesus said that the father "threw his arms around him and kissed him."

It's not too late because the Father wants you just the way you are. We think, *It's too late now. I don't have time to get cleaned up. I don't have time to get my life together.*

But the father loved the son as he was. He wasn't waiting for his son to get cleaned up and washed. He gave his sweaty, stinking, pig-sitting son a big bear hug, and the word for *kissed* here is the image of multiple kisses.

When you finally act, your heavenly Father comes running with arms wide open. He loves you just as you are, but He doesn't leave you that way. He puts His best robe on your dirty body. He puts the family ring on your hand. He kills the fattened calf.

Middle Eastern people of that day rarely, almost never, had meat for a meal. It was considered a rare delicacy. Occasionally it would be served for a party. So nothing was more extravagant than killing a fattened calf.

The focus of the story quickly shifted from the actions of the son to the actions of the father.

In our own lives, we make the story all about us, and it feels like it's too late. But the story is really about the Father.

AHA.

To conclude, I asked a friend of mine if I could share his AHA story.

Eight years ago I left home and went to Colorado State University. I was in a fraternity, and I majored in partying. For the first three semesters, I never stopped and thought about what I was doing. I wasn't praying at all. After three semesters, reality came crashing in on me. I could no longer deny what was happening. I had flunked four of my five classes. It was a wake-up call. I knew I needed to make some changes. I needed to get out of the fraternity and lose some of my friends, but what I really needed was to make a change in my relationship with God—if He would still have me.

In the frat house there was no place with privacy to make the phone call to my parents explaining that I had failed, so I took the phone into the bathroom. I remember there was a stack of pornography, and I didn't want to look in that direction, so I sat on top of it.

I called my parents and explained to them that I had blown it in a lot of areas of my life—not just my grades, but also in my walk with Christ. I had strayed from Him. And my parents listened to what I had to say, and then they said three words to me.

They didn't say, "Turn things around."

They didn't say, "Make things right."

They didn't say, "Get some help."

They didn't say, "Figure it out."

They didn't say, "We love you."

They didn't say, "We forgive you."

It was better than that.

What they said to me was:

"Just come home."

Chapter 13

LOST IN THE FATHER'S HOUSE—THE FINAL AHA

A young man walks down a long road. We can see he wears torn clothes; his sleeves are caked with mud.

The young man crests the horizon, plodding along. But suddenly the weary figure is blocked from view—another figure is running toward him.

This older man runs full tilt toward the younger man.

The two reach one another and embrace. The younger man, solemn faced and holding back tears, tries to communicate a grave message to the older man. The older man doesn't even seem to hear him—he kisses the young man, and tears of joy stream down his aged face. He looks back and calls to someone.

We see a courtyard filled with people. Tables are strewn about, along with a full spread of food. The guests aren't eating yet. Every eye is on a large table in a corner of the courtyard. The young man now wears a resplendent robe, and some color shows in his cheeks.

He smiles, watching as the older man, standing at the head of this table, addresses the crowd. He raises his cup.

Everybody in attendance raises their cups and toasts along with him, applauding after they drink.

After the Homecoming

The listeners heard Jesus tell of the celebration at the son's return to the father, and everyone listening assumed the story was over. I imagine Jesus finishing His sentence about the celebration and then pausing. The listeners would have nodded their heads, showing they were intrigued by this interesting story. Everyone likes a happy ending, right? To be fair, "So they began to celebrate" sounds an awful lot like, "and they lived happily ever after."

Then Jesus cleared His throat and used a classic transitional word in storytelling. He finished with the celebration scene everyone thought was the end of the story, and then Jesus said, "Meanwhile ..."

Attentive listeners might remember that Jesus began the story with a brief but important detail: "A man had two sons." After this opening sentence, the story focused completely on the younger son and the father. But when listeners came to the celebration scene, there was no older brother to be found.

Earlier that day, a man worked the ground tirelessly. He was the older brother, tending his father's lands faithfully. As the sun set on the field, the older brother heard a commotion at the family compound. He called out to a young servant to ask him what was going on. The servant excitedly explained about the return of the younger son and the father's celebration. At these words, the older brother was livid. Invited in by the servant, the older brother turned back to the field in refusal, dismissing the invitation coldly.

Later that evening, the father walked slowly toward the older brother in the field. As the father drew near to the older brother, he began to plead with him. The father entreated his older son, appealing him to celebrate the homecoming of his younger brother.

But here's how the older brother responded:

> But he answered his father, "Look! All these years I've been slaving for you and never disobeyed your orders. Yet you never gave me even a young goat so I could celebrate with my friends. But when this son of yours who has squandered your property with prostitutes comes home, you kill the fattened calf for him!"
>
> "My son," the father said, "you are always with me, and everything I have is yours. But we had to celebrate and be glad, because this brother of yours was dead and is alive again; he was lost and is found." (Luke 15:29–32)

Now don't miss this: the older brother never left the father, never broke the rules, never went to a distant country, *but he also never experienced AHA.* You have to ask yourself which story is more tragic—the younger son who lost everything and ended up in a pigpen but experienced AHA, or the older son who lived at home with the father and followed all the rules but never experienced AHA.

In fact, his speech revealed that he was disappointed in his father. His words revealed disgust for the extravagant grace shown to his younger brother. He demanded an explanation from his father. The older brother expected what some of the listeners of Jesus's parable were expecting: they wanted justice for the sinner.

Quandary of the Older Brother

To really understand the point of this parable, you have to look back at the beginning of the chapter. Luke 15:1 reads:

> Now the tax collectors and sinners were all gather-
> ing around to hear Jesus.

This is half of the audience for Jesus's parable. Spiritually speaking, these are the younger brothers. They are far from the Father, living in the Distant Country.

But they are not the only ones listening. Look at verse 2:

> But the Pharisees and the teachers of the law ...

So these are the older brothers.

The Pharisees and teachers of the Law spent their days steeped in study and clergy work. And here they were looking down on Jesus for spending time with the younger brothers.

So Jesus used the older brother in the parable to speak to them. He knew that the challenge of being an older brother was that you almost never saw yourself as the older brother. He created a character who had done everything right, a son who had been faithful and worked hard for the father's benefit. This is how many of the

Pharisees would have undoubtedly seen themselves. Spiritually speaking, these men literally worked in the Father's house—at the temple—but their hearts were far from Him.

Their understanding of God was flawed. They saw Him as harsh and unforgiving. A perspective like this sees God as a cosmic cop, patrolling the universe, waiting for folks to mess up so He can bust them and hand out an eternal verdict.

My brother-in-law is a police officer. Anyone related to a policeman knows that his or her work stories trump everyone else's. My story about discovering the original Greek word for *poop*[1] is never going to beat his story about rappelling down from a helicopter to incinerate illegally planted marijuana fields.

I remember one time he told me about some different accident scenes that he had come upon, including some with pretty serious injuries. As he told me about it, I said, "Well, they must have been relieved when you showed up on the scene. People must feel a lot better when they see you pull up."

He said, "Not really. A lot of times they're pretty nervous, because when I come on the scene, I'm there to investigate. I'm there to assign blame." He paused for a moment before adding, "But they're always glad to see the paramedics. See, the paramedics come in, and their job is to free those who are trapped, bandage those who have been wounded, and help those who are hurting."

The Pharisees listening to Jesus learned what we often forget: faithful followers of Christ aren't on earth to assign blame; we're

---

1   The word is *skubala*, by the way, used in Philippians 3:8.

here to free the trapped, bandage the wounded, help the hurting, and celebrate homecomings.

AHA.

The older son was indignant after seeing his father's actions. This older brother may have worked hard and faithfully tended the fields, but he was lost in his father's house.

There was no awakening.

There was no honesty.

There was no action.

The truth is, he, too, was a prodigal son. He, too, had a heart that was far from his father. He, too, was lost, but he didn't see it. Tim Keller put it this way, "The bad son was lost in his badness, but the good son was lost in his goodness."[2]

You may never have been to a Distant Country. You may have an impressive religious résumé. You may have followed all the rules. You may have read this entire book thinking of all the people you know in the Distant Country who really need to hear it. But I wonder if you are the one Jesus has been talking to all along.

Since older brothers have such a difficult time seeing themselves as someone in need of AHA—I know, I've been there—I want to give you a few descriptions of what an older brother is like:

Critical of others' sins

Older brothers often focus on the flaws of others. They're unwilling to recognize any repentance in prodigals, because they can't see

---

2   Tim Keller, *The Prodigal God* (New York: Penguin, 2008).

past the mistakes. So a person tries to make a truthful turnaround after living a life full of lies, and instead of being encouraging and supportive, an older brother will keep bringing up the lies they told before.

In being critical of others' sins, older brothers often have a hard time celebrating when AHA happens.

If you refuse to celebrate when your brothers and sisters come home from the Distant Country, it's a good indication that you're missing AHA in your own life and you're actually more lost than they are.

When someone comes home from the Distant Country who is repentant and broken and says they want to do things differently, the older brother will cross his arms instead of opening them. He might say things like, "Let's give it some time," or "Well, you're going to need to make some things right," or maybe, "Well, they need to get their act together."

Well, nobody asked you. This isn't your house. It's the *Father's* house. It's not for you to decide who gets to come home to be called sons and daughters. When there is a refusal to celebrate, it shows that we have missed the point. We've missed God's grace in our own life.

If we knew what we had been saved from, if we were aware of our lostness, if we could clearly see our sin—we would never be that way. We would be the first ones to celebrate. The Father would run, and we would run right behind Him, because we know what He's done for us. When I live with an awareness of what He's done for me—*oh man!*—my arms are wide open. But when we miss it, arms get crossed.

Confident in your goodness

A second indication of this older-brother syndrome is that there is a confidence in your own goodness instead of the Father's grace. Did you notice this? In verse 29, the older brother said to the father:

> "All these years I've been slaving for you and never disobeyed your orders."

What was he saying here? He was saying, "Look what I deserve. I've been good. I've followed the rules. I've done what you've asked me to. I deserve your blessing. I've earned it."

This kind of claim made no mention of the father's provision in his life. Like the Prodigal, the older brother had lived a life fully dependent on his father. But by saying this, he was unwilling even to acknowledge his father's generosity. Beyond that, his speech revealed a strain in his relationship with his father. He felt jilted by his father, complaining that he had never even received a small goat to have a party with his friends. How long had the older brother felt this way? I don't think these were brand-new feelings for him. After years of working hard for his father, he'd developed confidence in his own work ethic and discipline. His resentment probably started to grow when his father first gave the younger son half the inheritance. And he threw a party for the kid who blew a fortune on wild living?

This is the problem with confidence in our own goodness. We begin to believe we're going to earn something from the Father. But the Father's house is not a house of merit; it is a house of mercy.

While the older brother claims, "I've never disobeyed," the younger brother says, "I am not worthy." One brother appeals to his own merit. The other comes asking for mercy. One brother sulks in frustration; the other celebrates in joy.

Focusing on our own spiritual résumé divides our spiritual family. The father and Prodigal Son celebrate in the courtyard, and the older brother works alone in the field. God doesn't withhold mercy or stop the party just because one of His children disagrees. So until you go from "I've never disobeyed" to "I am not worthy," you will not have AHA.

Why Jesus Is So Hard on the Older Brothers

Look, I know this sounds harsh.

You may be reading this and thinking, *If Jesus is so merciful, why is He so tough on the Pharisees?* That's a fair question.

Here's what I think: Jesus knew that most people would base what they thought about God and what they thought God was like on how the Pharisees and teachers of the Law lived and behaved. It's even true today. The way employees interact with us sways what we think of the entire company. I mean, if you walk into a department store with your family and encounter a sales representative who is pushy in his pitch and uses foul language in front of your kids, you're not going to be happy. While you may take issue with him personally, what are you going to say? "I'd like to speak to the manager, please."

That's what was behind Jesus's challenge to these Pharisees. Jesus knew that because the older brothers lived and worked in the Father's house, people often looked to them for an accurate reference point of what the Father was like.

And there are a lot of older brothers totally misrepresenting the heart of God. They are the kind of people who portray God as the fathers we talked about in chapter one—a father who is unreasonable, unpleaseable, uncaring, and unmerciful. Often the older brothers' portrayal of God is what sends the prodigals to the Distant Country in the first place.

That's not the kind of Father we see in Luke 15.

The Final AHA

The father seeks out both sons

Both sons were in the wrong, and it was really both of their responsibilities to seek out their father. The younger son did this, eventually, but as soon as the father saw his son, he ran to him. He didn't sit back and wait for the boy, and he didn't posture himself as most patriarchs of that day would have—full of pride and indignant at any disrespect. No, he ran to his son.

When the older brother was in the field, the father left the celebration and went out to him. He engaged his son directly.

What does this tell us about God? God longs for a relationship with His children.

A friend of mine told me about an elderly man he knew who could no longer take care of himself and whose family made the difficult decision to put him in a nursing home. Every Sunday afternoon the man's daughter and her husband and their children would go see him. Every Sunday this elderly man would wait for his daughter and her family to come visit. He looked forward to it all week and was always out waiting for them. As the years passed, his mind grew weaker, and he soon had a hard time remembering his children's names. He would sometimes have a hard time getting back to his room.

But no matter what happened, on Sunday afternoon, he was always there waiting for his daughter and her family.

One day the daughter asked her father, "Daddy, do you know what day of the week it is?" The father couldn't tell her what day of the week it was. So the daughter said to her dad, "Well, Daddy, how did you know to wait for us today?"

The father replied, "Oh, honey, I wait for you every day."

God is a loving Father who longs for His children to come home. On the day you finally come home, you will find Him waiting for you. You might wonder, *How did He know to wait for me on this day? How did He know I was coming today?*

He has been waiting for you every day.

The father is loving and gracious to both sons

The father had every right to come down hard on both his sons. They deserved it. Those listening to this parable would have agreed that the father was well within his rights to deal out justice and punishment to both sons.

But after the younger son's insulting choices and reckless living, the father embraced him with kisses and hugs. And after the older brother's harsh words and disrespect, the father lovingly explained himself. The patriarch would never have had to explain himself in ancient times. Households were not democracies; they were dictatorships. Yet the father answered the older brother's anger with gentle patience and grace.

A pastor friend told me about a sixteen-year-old girl in his church who got pregnant. She was the daughter of a local businessman and church leader. She and her boyfriend went to the pastor because they were scared and didn't know what to do.

My friend asked her, "Have you told your father?"

She shook her head no. She said she was afraid of what he would do.

As time went by, she and her boyfriend continued to meet with the pastor, but she refused to tell her father. She knew she was beginning to show and couldn't keep it secret much longer, so she went to meet with the pastor one last time and told him her plan. She and her boyfriend were going to run away together. She asked the minister if he would tell her father the story after they were far enough away.

My pastor friend pleaded with her to tell her dad, but she was too scared. He insisted, "Let's go together right now and tell him. I will be by your side."

Before she had a chance to disagree, the minister ushered her out the door. They drove straight to her dad's office. His assistant said he was on the phone, but my friend told her, "I'm sorry, but this can't wait," and went right in with the girl. They sat down across from the father's desk. The father looked up, saw his daughter in tears and his pastor, and immediately said, "I'll call you back."

As soon as he hung up the phone, the girl started sobbing. She kept trying to speak, but the words wouldn't come out.

Finally the pastor said, "Your daughter has something she needs to tell you."

The father turned his gaze to his daughter, who wouldn't look at him. He breathed out with emotion and said, "I hope you are not here to tell me you're pregnant."

The girl sobbed even harder, choking out, "Daddy, I didn't mean to …"

My friend was a bit startled when the father suddenly sprang from his desk, came around it, and stood in front of his daughter. His voice bristling, he said, "You stand up! You stand up here and look me in the eye!"

She didn't move.

"I said stand up!" he said.

My friend was already on his feet, unsure of what would happen next.

The girl slowly stood up, and with tears streaming down her cheeks, she looked at her father.

Her father placed his hands on her shoulders and looked her square in the eyes. Then he spread out his arms and embraced his baby girl.

My friend was standing close enough that he heard what the father whispered into her ear, "It will be okay now, honey. I love you no matter what. We will get through this together."

We expect God to be an angry father who demands justice, but through Jesus, He gives us love and grace when we don't deserve it. Ultimately, the story in Luke 15 isn't about two sons who disobey. It is about a Father who loves His children unconditionally.

STUDY QUESTIONS

CHAPTER 1—THE DISTANT COUNTRY

1. Have you been to a Distant Country, or are you there now? What led you there?

2. What is your view of God? What are five to ten words you would use to describe how you honestly feel about Him?

3. When was that last time you simply said, "God, I need your help"?

PART 1—SUDDEN AWAKENING

CHAPTER 2—COMING TO YOUR SENSES

1. Why is it so difficult for us to hear and respond to the early warning alarms God puts in our lives?

2. Can you think of a time when you ignored an alarm and faced consequences later? Looking back, what should you have done to wake up instead of pressing Snooze?

3. Is there an alarm sounding in your life right now? What step(s) do you need to take to make sure you don't ignore it?

4. Pray for God to open your eyes to the ways He is trying to get your attention.

CHAPTER 3—A DESPERATE MOMENT

1. Have you ever hit rock bottom? What happened?

2. How have you responded to difficult circumstances in your life? Have they driven you *away from* God or drawn you *to* God?

3. Complete this sentence: "I stopped running from God when ..."

CHAPTER 4—A STARTLING REALIZATION

1. Have you had a moment of realization when you suddenly saw what had been right in front of you for a long time?

2. How much silence and solitude do you have in your life? How can you get more of that kind of time?

3. Do you have someone in your life who has your permission to "flip the switch," to tell you that last 5 percent of truth?

PART 2—BRUTAL HONESTY

CHAPTER 5—TALKING TO YOURSELF

1. When you look into the spiritual mirror, what do you see that no one else sees? What has kept you from bringing it into the light?

2. When you think about confession, what comes to mind?

3. Do you have someone in your life who asks you the hard questions and to whom you confess sin? What would it take for you to develop that kind of relationship?

4. What would change in your life if you were willing to regularly do the hard, uncomfortable work of confession?

CHAPTER 6—DENIAL: IF I IGNORE IT, MAYBE IT WILL GO AWAY

1. What happens to us when we live in denial?

2. When we are faced with uncomfortable truth, what are the emotions we experience that lead us to denial? How can we confront them rather than give in to them?

3. Read John 8:31–36. How does this relate to denial and confession?

CHAPTER 7–PROJECTION: IT'S NOT MY FAULT, SO IT'S NOT MY RESPONSIBILITY

1. Who or what do you tend to blame when you find yourself in "the pigpen"?

2. Why is it so difficult for us to accept fault—with no ifs, ands, or buts?

3. Is there someone you need to admit fault to right now? Write out what you need to say to them, and watch for projection and subtle ways you try to excuse yourself. Then go to them and read what you've written.

CHAPTER 8–MINIMIZE: IT'S NOT THAT BIG OF A DEAL

1. How do you see minimization in your life?

2. What is the connection between denial, projection, and minimization? Why do we so easily give in to these?

3. What can the response of the Ninevites in Jonah 3 teach us about a proper response to conviction?

4. The Prodigal Son realized that his decisions had caused significant relational damage that needed to be mended. Take a few minutes to honestly assess the relational consequences of your actions—even the actions that don't seem like that big of a deal. What can you start working on to mend those relationships?

PART 3—IMMEDIATE ACTION

CHAPTER 9—TIME TO GET UP

1. What are the barriers between brutal honesty and immediate action? Why is it so difficult to pass through them?

2. Why is there often such a difference between "public beliefs," "private beliefs," and "core beliefs"? How can we begin to develop consistency?

3. As you've read through this book so far, maybe you've had a sudden awakening, and maybe even been brutally honest with yourself. In light of that, what action do you need to take?

4. What is standing between you and that necessary action?

CHAPTER 10—PASSIVITY: I'M SURE EVERYTHING WILL WORK ITSELF OUT

1. It seems so natural to choose the path of least resistance, but that's not what will lead us to AHA. How does the hard work of

immediate action bring changes that the path of least resistance never could?

2. Passivity happens when we honor something over God. We rarely, if ever, intend for that to happen, so what leads us to honoring things like family, money, and comfort above God?

3. What's your "first step"? How will you act on it?

CHAPTER 11—PROCRASTINATION: I'LL GET TO IT LATER

1. What are the areas of life where you procrastinate?

2. If you look back honestly, what has procrastination cost you?

3. How do you see putting off the pain, prolonging the pleasure, and/or planning it to perfection playing a role in your procrastination?

4. Can you think back to some "here and now" moments you've experienced in the past? What led to those moments, and what changes came out of them?

CHAPTER 12—DEFEATISM: IT'S TOO LATE NOW

1. Do you feel, or have you felt, that it's too late for you? Why?

2. When has your life been like trying to plug up the hole in the bottom of a pool—the more you try to fix something, the worse it gets?

3. Have you tried to make changes before that either didn't work or didn't last long? Look back through the list of questions on pages 189 and 190. Were any of those true of you?

4. What needs to be different this time if you're truly going to experience AHA?

CHAPTER 13—LOST IN THE FATHER'S HOUSE: THE FINAL AHA

1. Do you find it easy or difficult to accept "prodigals" when they return home?

2. Knowing what we know about the older brother from the end of the story, can you understand his response to his brother's actions?

3. From what we've learned about AHA, what are the next steps the older brother needs to take in order to experience AHA?

4. Whether you are more of a younger brother or an older brother right now, what are your next steps toward experiencing AHA?

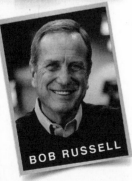

Not a Fan

Becoming a Completely Committed Follower of Jesus

Kyle Idleman

Are you a follower of Jesus? Don't answer too quickly. In fact, you may want to read this book before you answer at all. Consider it a "define the relationship" conversation to determine exactly where you stand. You may indeed be a passionate, fully devoted follower of Jesus. Or you may be just a fan who admires Jesus but isn't ready to let him cramp your style. Then again, maybe you're not into Jesus, period. In any case, don't take the question, Are you a follower of Jesus? lightly. Some people don't know what they've said yes to, and other people don't realize what they've said no to, says Pastor Kyle Idleman. But Jesus is ready to clearly define the relationship he wants with his followers. *Not a Fan* calls you to consider the demands and rewards of being a true disciple. With frankness sprinkled with humor, Idleman invites you to live the way Jesus lived, love the way Jesus loved, pray the way Jesus prayed, and never give up living for the one who gave his all for you.

Available in stores and online!

Gods at War

Defeating the Idols that Battle for Your Heart

Kyle Idleman

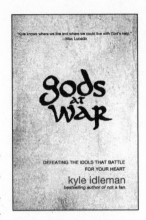

In *gods at war*, Kyle Idleman, bestselling author of *not a fan*, helps every believer recognize there are false gods at war within each of us, and they battle for the place of glory and con-trol in our lives. What keeps us from truly following Jesus is that our hearts are pursuing something or someone else. While these pursuits may not be the "graven images" of old, they are in fact modern day idols. Behind the sin you're struggling with, the discouragement you're dealing with, the lack of purpose you're living with is a false god that is winning the war for your heart.

According to Idleman, idolatry isn't an issue — it is the issue.

By asking insightful questions, Idleman reveals which false gods each of us are allowing on the throne of our lives. What do you sac-rifice for? What makes you mad? What do you worry about? Whose applause do you long for? We're all wired for worship, but we often end up valuing and honoring the idols of money, sex, food, romance, success and many others that keep us from the intimate relationship with God that we desire.

Using true, powerful and honest testimonies of those who have struggled in each area, *gods at war* illustrates a clear path away from the heartache of our 21st century idolatry back to the heart of God — enabling us to truly be completely committed followers of Jesus.

Available in stores and online!

ZONDERVAN®
.com

JOIN THE CONVERSATION

Tell your friends, share quotes, ask questions, discuss the book, discover extra resources:

#AHAbook

CONNECT WITH KYLE IDLEMAN